Elizabeth Swados

AT PLAY

Elizabeth Swados has composed, written, and directed more than thirty theater pieces, including *The Trilogy, Nightclub Cantata, Runaways, Alice in Concert, Doonesbury, Rap Master Ronnie, The Haggadah, Jonah, Job, Esther, Jerusalem* (with Yehudah Amichai), *The 49 Years,* and *Missionaries.* She has performed at La MaMa, The Public Theater, The Manhattan Theatre Club, The Brooklyn Academy of Music, Carnegie Hall, and other theaters on Broadway, Off-Broadway, and all over the world. Ms. Swados has composed music for film and television as well as a song cycle, *Bible Women,* which has toured the United States. She has published a memoir, novels, nonfiction books, and children's books.

Her newest work includes a musical theater piece about the life and work of Alfred Jarry, which premiered at the Flea Theater in February 2005 and opens at the Alley Theatre in Houston in September 2007. In the summer of 2005 she created a musical theater piece in collaboration with a cast of students about attending New York University and living in the city, which was performed for the incoming freshmen at NYU. The twenty-fifth anniversary concert of *Missionaries* was performed at the Cathedral of St. John the Divine in December 2005. *My Depression: A Picture Book* was published in April 2005. She is a faculty member at NYU's Tisch School of the Arts and lives in New York City.

ALSO BY ELIZABETH SWADOS

———

NOVELS

Leah and Lazar
The Myth Man
Flamboyant

NONFICTION

The Four of Us
Listening Out Loud
My Depression: A Picture Book

CHILDREN'S BOOKS

The Girl with the Incredible Feeling
Lullaby (with Faith Hubley)
Skydance (with Faith Hubley)
Inside Out
Dreamtective
Hey You! C'mere
The Animal Rescue Store

PLAYS

Runaways
The Red Sneaks
Alice in Concert
The Haggadah
Jewish Girlz

AT PLAY

AT PLAY

TEACHING

TEENAGERS

THEATER

Elizabeth Swados

FABER AND FABER, INC.

AN AFFILIATE OF FARRAR, STRAUS AND GIROUX

NEW YORK

Faber and Faber, Inc.
An affiliate of Farrar, Straus and Giroux
19 Union Square West, New York 10003

Grateful acknowledgment is made for permission to reprint the following previously published material:

Excerpts from "I Whistle A Happy Tune" by Richard Rodgers and Oscar Hammerstein II, copyright © 1951, and "In My Own Little Corner" and "Ten Minutes Ago," copyright © 1957 by Richard Rodgers and Oscar Hammerstein II. All rights owned and administered by Williamson Music. Copyright renewed. International copyright secured. Used by permission. All rights reserved.

Excerpts from *Jewish Girlz*, *The Red Sneaks*, and *Runaways* by Elizabeth Swados used by permission of Samuel French, Inc. All rights reserved.

Library of Congress Cataloging-in-Publication Data
Swados, Elizabeth.
    At play ; teaching teenagers theater / by Elizabeth Swados.— 1st ed.
    p. cm.
    ISBN-13: 978-0-571-21120-3 (pbk. : alk. paper)
    ISBN-10: 0-571-21120-8 (pbk. : alk. paper)
    1. Theater—Study and teaching (Secondary).   2. Improvisation
(Acting).   I. Title.

PN2075.S87 2006
792.071'2—dc22

                                                2005032804

Designed by Cassandra J. Pappas

www.fsgbooks.com

1   3   5   7   9   10   8   6   4   2

Dedicated to:

Henry Brant
Ellen Stewart
Andrei Serban
Peter Brook
and
Joseph Papp

My great teachers

CONTENTS

ACKNOWLEDGMENTS

A special thank you to Nicola Barber for her help in organizing and designing the look of these pages as well as for being a generous friend.

And to Elna Baker for continuous support and typing.

And to all the casts of *Runaways*, *The Red Sneaks*, *Swing*, *Hating Pot*, *New Americans*, and *Loss and Gain*—grown and young—who taught me how to teach.

Thanks to my patient editor, Linda Rosenberg.

GAIN OF COURAGE

Forty-two Seconds till Game was over. The crowd in the stands chanting "Knights, Knights, Knights." I Didn't know this football game will be so big to everybody. Me, Myself standing on the side-line with a big fear that we will lose. Score was 32–27. All we needed was a touchdown to win the game. I needed to go in the game and do something but I was scared. All I was thinking what would happen if I drop it, what would happen if time ran out, what would happen if I slip and fall. So many things in my head would not let me concentrate. I had to do something. I was the only receiver they had not put in the game. Then suddenly Coach told me "you're in." I was terri-fied to see the coach talking to me, But I was scared and said No, I can't, but there was no choice, I had to get in the game and win it for my team, and so I did. I didn't care if I made a mistake, all I needed to know was that I can do this. So I waited patiently till the ball was snapped to the quarterback, then I ran rapidly to the touchdown area and I was wide open and suddenly I see the ball being passed down my way and I opened my arms and "I catched it, I catched it." The crowd then suddenly cheered with great emotion. All I could be thinking at that moment was that I had the courage to step on the field and make something happen. DAMN, All this time I didn't know that I could make a difference.

—Pierre, age fifteen, in *Loss and Gain*,
performed in 2004 for Hospital Audiences, Inc.

HOW TO USE THIS BOOK

I've written this book to share some of the techniques and exercises I've used for more than twenty-five years with young actors. The typical age range for my work spans from twelve to the early twenties, and I usually put all the ages together so that everyone learns from one another. Most often, I concentrate on young people in middle and high school. While I create shows independently of schools, I wrote this book with the intention of assisting teachers in creating theater with their students. After a year of workshops, my company of young people creates a custom-made piece for our ensemble. In the same way, a teacher and class may create an original piece after working together for all or part of the school year. And just as my young company performs in front of peers at public and private schools and community centers as well as juvenile and psychiatric facilities, groups of students could perform before fellow students. Therefore you will note that I often write about a series of exercises that have been put together to help create a show. But please be aware that the exercises I've chosen can and do serve several other categories of theatrical experience as well:

1. To make a show outside of school

2. To make a show in school

3. To train young actors in a community or drama school environment

4. To train young actors in a classroom or after-school environment

5. To use one or two exercises in a limited class time

The exercises themselves have been grouped in several categories. You should find your own way of using these categories. If you have students working with you over a long period of time and intend to create something with them, you can use the order suggested by this book. Or you can improvise from it. If you want to make a show but have only three weeks, you can decide what you need from this book and extract it accordingly. If you simply want to teach in the classroom, you can use the exercises randomly as they suit the class. Each exercise is aimed toward a specific part of the theater student's development and works very well in tandem with other exercises and theater games. I advise you to adhere strictly to only one rule: make the time that you work separate, individual, and sacred. If there is one resounding note in my work, it is that young people should know that the theater can be theirs and that they can find a new language that can define the future of the art and its audience, and provide a personal, exciting way to express themselves. An unusual mode of expression for theater is like nothing else.

A final note: I tend to mention musical theater more than plays because my inclination is toward work with music. You don't have to be a musician or singer to do theater. On the other hand don't rule out any art or area of research when dreaming about your participation. Let your talents roam free. There are too many specialists in the world of theater, too many categories and methods and rules. You will find your place and your own voice. But for now try everything.

INTRODUCTION: MY STORY

I think of myself lying wide awake in my pink-and-white bedroom in a restored Victorian house in Buffalo, New York. We lived near the zoo, and I grew up imitating elephant calls and the screeches of peacocks. I also hear strains of a song called "Try to Remember" wafting up the stairway like the smell of crisp toast. My father is at the piano, crooning this melancholy song from *The Fantasticks* (a story of lovers separated by a wall, based on the legend of Pyramus and Thisbe). My brother is in his messy rat's nest of a room listening to "Bali Hai" from *South Pacific*. His record player is turned up high and he is braying along like a proud donkey. My mother sits at the kitchen table, a cigarette in one hand, a drink in the other, reciting "The calla lilies are in bloom agayne" in a semi-British, tight-jawed accent. She dreams of being Katharine Hepburn.

My childhood home was a theater. We were all dramatic. We made grand entrances and exits. Quotes from Shakespeare at the dinner table were as normal as "Pass the potatoes." I remember drowsing off to the mumbles of my parents helping each other learn lines. When I was four or five, I sat tucked into a rear seat of Buffalo's Studio Arena Theater, where I got to watch my parents star in a play called *Picnic*. My mother looked so tall and elegant in her gray shirt-dress and spike heels. She also wore a black beret. I was overjoyed. My mother, a beatnik! But at some crux of the play, she became fiercely angry. And as I sat in my seat, she tore the shirt off a man named Hal. He was handsome, with big arms and blond chest hair. I didn't understand why my mother did that. Scream and tear a man's shirt off? I burst into tears as she squinted her eyes and puffed at her cigarette. This was nothing like the mother I knew. I had to be carried into the green room behind the stage area because I was sobbing so loudly.

After the show, my mother sat me on her lap and laughingly explained that she was just "acting." There was no "just" as far as I was concerned. I could smell the heavy powder on her face; her eyebrows appeared to have been replaced by painted lines. I wouldn't touch her hands. Those long red fingernails had torn off Hal's shirt! I didn't understand this concept of "acting." It was happening, but not really happening? Her fury was "part of the play"? I calmed down but remained on guard; there was no telling what this woman who had been my mother would do. She washed her painted eyebrows off and began to look more familiar. On the way home, my father tried to reassure me that "acting" was very common and that lots of people put on plays and went home and watched Jack Paar like everyone else. (Jack Paar was the first Jay Leno.) In another scene of this *Picnic*, my father backed off from marrying my mother and left her alone. I found his refusal confusing since I was sure I'd seen the movies of their wedding several times. I watched them very carefully in the days to come. When I saw that they sat together at the dinner table and cuddled side by side in our large Buick convertible, I still didn't understand the concept of acting. They told me again and again, acting was pretending. It wasn't the real thing. I never believed them fully. Theater was that convincing.

Soon I was initiated into the family madness. My brother Lincoln directed me in his two-person adaptation of Rodgers and Hammerstein's *Cinderella*. I was cast as Cinderella; he played all the other parts. His version lasted less than ten minutes, but I got to sing the lines "In my own little corner in my own little chair / I can be whatever I want to be." I think that's all he let me sing at the time, but I relished my moment. I savored the triumph over my nasty stepsisters (whom he played) when he placed the golden sneakers on my feet and when I won the heart of the prince (my brother again). I truly fell for him when he danced me in a slow waltz and sang, "Ten minutes ago I saw you / I looked up when you came through the door / My head started reeling / You gave me the feeling the room had no ceiling or floor." My parents, as well as Ducky and Howard Newman, the couple who lived downstairs, applauded and whistled and cheered. My mother had a piercing whistle (she'd been a tomboy) and my father shouted "Bravo! Bravo!" like an operagoer. They hugged us as if we'd won first prize in some spectacular contest.

I mark that as the first time I realized that singing and talking and moving my arms up and down put me on the plus side of the human scoreboard. I didn't think I was "acting." I truly believed I'd been a poor adopted orphan. (I'd always wanted to be adopted, it seemed dramatic.) I knew I'd been transformed into a princess. I knew I loved Cinderella when I danced in my brother's arms. And I know it now. Theater has never been a "made-up world" for me. It's always been a place where in a moment you can be transformed into another reality. The word *pretend* reminds me of telling white lies—it's neither here nor there. No spine.

I had my secret ambitions and dreams. I memorized most of the words to the Rodgers and Hammerstein and Rodgers and Hart musicals. I lay on my bed and sang along and became Anna in *The King and I*, Sarah in *Guys and Dolls*, and Marian in *The Music Man*. I'd never seen those musicals—or any musical, for that matter—and had little notion of their stories. I made up plots by looking at the photos on the album cover. I was probably completely off base, but I often moved myself to fake tears. By the time I was nine or ten and saw my first real musical on Broadway, I'd already "written" (in my own mind) most of the great musical masterpieces of all time. My whole grammar school was in awe. Despite those fantasies, the first time I saw a real Broadway musical, I screamed my lungs out at the end in wild happiness. I'd never felt such joy. The voices were angelic; the lights came from heaven; the sets moved. Great dancers tapped and kicked and they did so at exactly the same time. I was overcome.

Julie Andrews in *The Boyfriend* was a revelation. Musicals were better and bigger than life. I didn't remember the names of the characters, their stories or problems, but I saw a whole world come to life onstage. A singing, dancing, speaking, feeling extravaganza of life. Life just became—well—so *alive*. So much brighter and stronger than my bedroom in Buffalo. I didn't understand why people couldn't live in musicals all the time. Speaking loudly, bursting into song, running offstage, running onstage, changing costumes, jumping over sets, tap dancing, spinning. Yes! Why wasn't there more tap dancing in the streets of Buffalo, New York? I knew then that the volume, speed, and intensity of daily life weren't going to be enough for me. I was going to turn up the sound and shine a brighter light on the earth and persuade everyone to sing along. I'd stage my musicals on Main Street. I'd star in them too. My dreams went on a rampage, my narcissism went a bit out of control. Did I want to sing, act, dance, write? (Did I even know what directing was?) I never differentiated. I just wanted to *make* theater. In second grade I directed my first show. It was about the great pumpkin on Halloween. I forced all my friends to follow me into the basement, where I had costumes and a script ready. My plans were sabotaged when one girl refused to put a hollowed-out, stinky, seed-filled pumpkin over her head.

As I grew into my high school years, those dreams, though still persistent, became very complicated. The world in which I was growing up had changed. Some of my new perspectives evolved from my simply becoming more mature. Then came the problems of family and adolescence. My family and friends suffered through different kinds of social and personal upheaval. I was highly aware, like other young people, that the sixties were supposed to be a radical decade. There was a new edge and fire in our country. The "lead characters" that inspired me didn't tap dance or wear hoop skirts; the story lines were rarely about finding one's sweetheart in the midst of adversity. My attention was turned from the victories of the past to the multiple injustices of the present. Sweet choruses and waltzing couples didn't fit into the world of civil rights conflicts and assassinations. How could the stage compete with the lives and deaths of Martin Luther King, Jr., and the Kennedys? I still vividly remember the horse with no rider and boots hung upside down from the stirrups trotting slowly down Pennsylvania Avenue. This was the "theater" of President Kennedy's funeral. The stage couldn't compare to the civil rights marches taking place in Mississippi and the bombing of a church with four little girls inside. The images were unforgettable. Now, unfortunately, we see violent deaths and memorials every day, and to some they are an odd kind of entertainment.

I was especially influenced by Bob Dylan. No one had written lyrics like his before—both poetic and political. In my young mind, musical theater became irrelevant in comparison to Dylan's songs. (I still believe Bob Dylan is one of our great poets.) The Beatles created theater for the ears with their unusual harmonies and sorcerers' voices. Every broadcast of their concerts, as well as reports of their antics and love affairs, became my theater. In clubs multicolored lights and flashing strobes became the theatrical lighting. And no playwright or actor had the energy of a psychedelic rock band, the guitar riffs of George Harrison, or the pounding drums of Cream. Well, not to me anyway. The theater had fallen in my estimation. It was a place where my parents went to watch people in heavy makeup talking to one another in phony voices about silly little problems. I was hardly interested. Instead, I got myself a guitar and plunked away until my fingers bled.

I tried to imitate Richie Havens's merciless rhythmic strumming. I wrote many, many sad and angry songs. Some of them were good; some were just awful. I listened to Joni Mitchell and Joan Baez and I feverishly copied down chords and lyrics. Folk and rock music was theater for me.

NOW, YOU MAY be thinking, "Please don't tell me about the sixties. I'm tired of the sixties. Hippies were potheads and radicals were boring." I understand. There were aspects to the sixties that seem silly or bizarre now. But it was also a time when you could take huge risks and lay out your own path. The reason I mention this decade is that it was when I was a teenager. At that time, there were no shows or plays designed to include my generation in theater. There was no recognition of my inner turmoil or the urgency I felt. There were no theater songs that reflected the turbulent atmosphere in our country.

During my high school years I turned my back on most theater, but I did encounter one show that stirred my imagination and gave me a hint of what could satisfy my evolving tastes. The musical/play was from England and was called *Oh What a Lovely War*. The tone was satirical and dangerous. The subject was ostensibly World War I, but the images and words evoked all war. And, in a very entertaining way, the actors let us know the absolute horror and absurdity of war. There was no real plot to the piece, but it moved and grew in intensity like a song. The music itself was in the old style of the British music hall, but the players distorted it (as the Beatles did on their *Sgt. Pepper* album) and made fun of the tunes. In a flash, however, the sounds could become very scary or sad, and I liked this combination of humor and danger. The soldiers acted like buffoons on the stage. They marched drunkenly in a circle and fell over one another, becoming caricatures of military men. Simultaneously, terrible scenes from World War I were projected on a large screen in the back. I was laughing and feeling a sense of horror at the same time. I learned about the creators' disgust for war but there was no preachiness, for much of the emotional information was displayed through the body and sounds.

At that time, I could be moved by a physical language much more than naturalistic chatter onstage. *Oh What a Lovely War* was a good example of this: it was edgy and didn't belong in the conventional categories of either drama or musical theater. I believed that what I was seeing was something I'd like to do: combine music, theater, and politics to entertain and trouble the audience, never let it off the hook. Also, *Oh What a Lovely War* had been put together by a collective of actors who worked with the writer and director, and the unique teamlike spirit could be felt by the audience. This was a whole new concept in comparison with the traditional system of "lead parts" and "stars." Plus, the director of *Oh What a Lovely War* was a woman; her name was Joan Littlewood. I imagined she was tough and resourceful. At that time, women didn't often direct—and certainly not musical theater.

In my junior year of high school I was tutoring low-income students in English and not doing it very well. I couldn't sustain my young students' attention. Out of desperation I abandoned the books and began to make theater with them. I don't remember exactly what we created; perhaps it was awful. But attendance at my class grew and all of us seemed to thrive on making a play. It became a means of expression for those who didn't quite fit in, since making theater can be a way of using the body and voice to talk about problems. You can talk about them without revealing embarrassing details. You can use characters and metaphors to reveal hidden aspects of yourself. I found that theater games and improvisations helped liberate us from our stiff self-conscious adolescent turmoil. We all felt like outsiders — but each adrift in a different way.

I later attended Bennington College. I found that it was a haven for young people who wanted to be painters, writers, composers, dancers, and performers. Everywhere you turned there was a pottery wheel or a tall steel sculpture, someone playing a violin out the window or reading a poem on the great commons lawn. Dancers stretched at their barre on dining room tables during meals. A class practiced guerrilla theater by taking over a dormitory. This was a fabulous, eye-opening environment for a young person like me, though I admit it would have been less precious if it had included some math or history. Even though we were encouraged by advisers to take academic classes seriously, most of the students spent their time creating original works, with the result that, if you got too serious, you could suffocate from self-involvement. You could also create trash, telling yourself it was "artistic." I remember a concert where the performer said the word *yes* over and over again in hundreds of intonations for over an hour. To this day I have no idea whether it was an ingenious concept or a version of "The Emperor's New Clothes." Later that year the same man sang the telephone book. (Let me assure you that there was also much work done on classics — Shakespeare, Chaucer. We didn't paint canvases with hair full time!)

What made Bennington special was that we could try *anything*. It was a laboratory where we were invited to be creative and courageous. My first mentor was a highly original, intense composer and arranger by the name of Henry Brant. He orchestrated giant movie scores — he'd worked on the epic Taylor and Burton *Cleopatra*, for instance — and taught music from a theatrical point of view. He viewed instruments as characters and referred to his symphonies as "battles or circuses." He encouraged me to create my own musical dramas all over the campus. His special interest was in how to use space—for example, thirty years ago he had a musician climb a tall ladder . . . while playing the flute. Simultaneously he'd position a cellist down the hill. As a vocalist I was instructed to sing from a tree. A violinist was to lie in a meadow and play. Then, as a signal, he'd turn on a flashlight and we'd all start playing, shouting, or singing at once. Sometimes it was chaos, but when you heard one of his flute melodies from a distance, it might have been a voice coming from another world. He also encouraged us to tune instruments differently than they were supposed to be tuned, and to create original instruments out of round saw blades. He believed that the performance of music should be its own form of theater. He also believed musicians should learn how to use language as music, so he encouraged us to write words instead of notes whenever we wanted. This was when I began to realize that monologues, dialogues, and spoken passages had their own music. I began to understand the importance of dynamics, and the incredible range of consonants and vowels.

Henry was ahead of his time, and I got the benefit of his vision. I now see his ideas all around me. Entire theaters have been renovated to create unusual, run-down, and open atmospheres for performances. If you attend a Shakespeare performance outdoors, chances are the play you are seeing will take place all around you, not just on a proscenium stage. Knowing every aspect of a space and using the crooks and corners imaginatively is a crucial part of directing. In rock and roll as well as avant-garde classical music, instrumentalists are acting, moving, and finding new theatrical ways to play their instruments.

I left Bennington several times, though I loved the school (and I did ultimately get a B.A.). But the atmosphere seemed too cloistered for me when young people were protesting all over the country. The Vietnam War and the tragic shooting of protesting students at Kent State, Ohio, made me want to be more active and urban. As a result, several friends of mine and I put together a "radical" theater company: the Fusion Theater. During the time of the most intense protests against Vietnam, we conceived of a show that included carrying a coffin through the audience as well as choreography in which the whole company died onstage (several times). We played in coffeehouses, common rooms, and cafeterias transformed into theater spaces. When I look back on the Fusion Theater now, our artistic choices seem a bit heavy-handed, but I'm proud that, as sophomores in college, we wrote, rehearsed, and booked a tour for ourselves around the East Coast. I believe that high school students can make their own theater groups too. If they're excited enough to form garage bands, become Olympic runners, excel in science, and write phenomenal poetry, they can certainly find their own theatrical voices.

The theater has to take young people seriously. I don't understand why there aren't teenage ensembles and small homemade theaters that young people make themselves. You don't need money. We'll go into the notion of "poor theater"—theater made with nothing—later. I don't encourage young actors to drop out of high school or college. To create believable theater, you must have experiences, but a strong background in other sciences and arts can only broaden your range. Knowledge is important because it's the small, specific memories that make each play or performance unique.

In my college years, I was exposed to a very physically oriented kind of acting. A Polish director, Jerzy Grotowski, was developing exercises influenced by gymnastics and yoga. Suddenly every actor, director, and writer I knew was standing on his or her head and rolling into double somersaults. Grotowski was one of the directors who introduced the notion of a circuslike physicality into theater techniques and performance. Before then much theater was "naturalistic," meaning that actors worked more internally and spoke in everyday voices. Shakespeare and Greek dramas were exceptions to this, but modern theater was acted much as if the actors were on *Law & Order* or *CSI*: real people dealing with recognizable problems. The new theater, of which I became a part, was not as interested in the day-to-day domestic troubles as it was in larger-than-life myths and ritualistic spectacle. Today we know how the whole body can create enormous energy and character in hip-hop and break dancing; the moves reflect a collective emotion. But in the late 1970s, this new style of theater changed my life, because within it I could explore sound and rhythm, poetry and politics, harmony, dramatic noise, and athletic movement. During my third year at Bennington, I began to bring sound, new rhythms, and music from other cultures into plays. I was lucky to be brought to New York by a series of teachers and graduate directors, and I ended up working in the place that became my first professional home.

There was a small building at 474A East Fourth Street called the La MaMa Experimental Theatre Company. Ellen Stewart, the "Mama," specialized in bringing artists from all over the world to work together. I took a low-paying job as a composer/gofer for a Belgian director who had been my teacher and who was making a new show at La MaMa during the summer. I don't remember much about it except that it was about Quasimodo—only there were five Quasimodos and they kept changing places for reasons I did not quite understand. Ms. Stewart watched me work and "beeped" me. When Ellen Stewart "beeps" a person, you become her baby. And she has hundreds, if not thousands, of babies all over the world. A baby is any style of artist or person who moves the heart and imagination of Mama. You remain a baby through your whole life and inherit an international population of brothers and sisters.

Ellen Stewart introduced me to theater artists from such countries as Argentina, Japan, Israel, Morocco, Lebanon, Korea, the Philippines, and several African nations. I got to study with a Native American theater group as well as with actors and directors from La MaMa satellites in France, Germany, and Holland. I lived in a whirlwind of music, movement, and language. I was invited to collaborate on the music for some shows, and to observe many others. At La MaMa I began to realize that there was a common thread in international theater: storytelling. There are many stories whose roots have been passed down through generations in both families and culture. The ancient art of acting out and telling stories is the core of most theater, but at La MaMa stories weren't told just with words but in new and experimental styles. The international groups with which I worked were telling their stories in ways that I had mostly never seen. Puppetry and masks. Fire. Animal language. Gymnastics. Audience confrontation. Multimedia. Commedia dell'arte. I became part of a community of actors, writers, and directors who saw the audience members as partners and often placed them in the middle of the drama. The sixties and early seventies were the time when rules were broken and the "fourth wall"—the wall between audience and actors—crumbled completely.

From the age of nineteen to my midtwenties I traveled with and learned much from theater in other countries. Many young artists were trying to create a universal language of sound, movement, and character archetypes—using the forces of the psyche through which all human beings could create and share theater. Whether we knew the same stories or not, we shared the forces that created our dreams and nightmares. We had similar conflicts. During this part of my life, I acquired the grounding for my theatrical life. I was in graduate school, but I was learning by working. I was a part of shows that traveled from city to city, town to town, village to village. Not only did I get to see many masters of the theater at work, but I saw their equals in shamans, priests, storytellers, and dancers in African and Middle Eastern countries. My lessons during those years are the foundation for what I will talk about in this book. When you see amazing performances, you want to know what it is that stirred you. I will tell you about many of my experiences and how I transformed what I saw into what I made and taught—how these ancient and foreign sensibilities can help us create new forms of theater ourselves.

These ideas shouldn't be mysterious or odd to you. There's a musical movement that's been around for several decades, brought into focus by Peter Gabriel, Mickey Hart, and Paul Simon, which introduces African and Indian rhythms into rhythm and blues. Moby has recorded a cappella blues mixed with electronic sound. South African music has been sung chorally behind Paul Simon's rock songs. Middle Eastern drumming has been juxtaposed with ancient Gregorian chant, Celtic ballads with Kodo—a Japanese group of drummers. Today there are labels for various experiments in world music. Imagine these cross-cultural musical recipes with stories, movement, and acting. Imagine young actors who can move expertly and also make sounds and music, and, through this, touch the power of the unconscious by what they do. This is what my international experience brought to me, and I'm going to hone it down and try to explain it to you.

I learned a lifetime of skills during those years. And I also learned that the specific ideas I learned about voice, movement and storytelling could be applied to multicultural casts in America. The American landscape is full of diverse, conflicting "tribes," and when I returned from my travels, I decided to devote my work to a kind of street theater, a political storytelling theater that could speak to the young people in the village of the United States. Maybe I was naive, but I thought theater could change opinions and expose injustices. I had missed the brash street sounds of American music and writing while I was abroad . . . the up-front, rude, edgy quality of rebellious young people . . . the confrontational loudmouths of downtown theater. The times called for raw emotions and urban clashes. The youthful anger I'd felt during college had been put on hold, but when I returned to the States, I found there was so much still to be angry about. In doing my international work I'd rarely used English. Now I had the itch to yell in my native tongue for and about the victims of unjust policies, poverty, and racism. This kind of political attitude is not as popular now as it was in 1978, but I believe that it's just as necessary, as the state of world politics today becomes increasingly incomprehensible. I'm not being pedantic—you don't have to be into politics to make theater. I'm speaking for myself. For others, there are as many subjects, characters, and stories as there are people on this earth.

Still, like many young people of any era, I had passion but I didn't know how to focus it. I began to watch and listen to the neighborhoods and streets. I witnessed and experienced the isolation of other young people. I still wrote music for other directors' shows but I found myself roaming, looking for what I wanted to tell, for I had to find a theme that matched my passion to my needs. I came back at a time when record numbers of runaways were on the streets of our cities. Kids seemed to be drifting into New York with ambitious dreams. I'd been a runaway myself at one time, so I felt strong empathy for the hungry young street kids. I saw how the effects of a bad home could create so many variations. I began to approach kids, those from age ten or eleven to their early twenties. I listened to their stories about the abuse adults had laid on them; I heard about the lives of those who had left their homes and those who wanted to. At that time, adults had all the power, and there weren't even the channels—such as you have today—to vent or explore despair. I believed it was time to draw attention to the fact that America didn't seem to like its children (even though I was to learn quickly that it was a little ambitious to address America as a whole). I knew I wanted to make a show about the runaways I was meeting during my wanderings and the runaways I knew from my own life. I needed to speak for the runaway I knew best—which was me. My work at La MaMa gave me enough of a résumé to be able to present my idea to the few producers who graciously took the time to hear me, though I was turned down many times. People said it was "too much of a downer" and I should "show them a script with a hopeful character." The more I was rejected, the more energized I became. Finally, after a long, intense meeting, I convinced a street-smart producer named Joseph Papp to back me up. He gave me money and a space—which was a miracle I have never taken for granted.

Joseph Papp wasn't like anyone I'd met before. He was, in many ways, a combination of a fast-talking salesman, a rabbi, and a quick-change artist. He was a rough, brown-eyed angel; his thoughts sped from idea to idea; he seemed to fear nothing. If he liked an idea, he went for it. He rarely cared about the risks involved or the opinions of others. He said he'd pay for a cast; more important, he put his reputation on the line. This kind of backing of a twenty-six-year-old who hadn't even written her play yet is practically unheard of. But Joe Papp was one of a kind—and another remarkable mentor. He understood me in a way no one else ever had. He not only had respect for my creative aims, but he also had compassion for the ups and downs of young lives. Joe is another person who inspired me to fight for young people. I told him I didn't want to use actors, for I still mistrusted actors—American actors. I thought they were phony. Also, I was against the idea of adults playing kids. I especially despised it when adults pretended to be sad teenagers. They tried so hard to be cute or cool and melodramatic. Most adult actors have no idea how to behave like a messed-up kid. I told Joe Papp I had to do the show with real kids and, in some cases, real runaways. "Okay, Swados," he said to me, "just don't burn down the building." This was such a lucky moment for me. Would I have been able to do the show if he'd turned me down? I like to think I'd have found a way, but Joe was my cigar-smoking, Yiddish-speaking angel. And that was my first and last miracle. From then on it was all hard work.

And now begins the part of my story that corresponds most directly to what I hope to convey in this book. I will describe, step by step, how a group of young people, aged eight to twenty-one, came together and created a musical theater piece about their dangerous world and its small redemptions. What we did was remarkable in its way, but the most amazing part was that we did it at all. I think the cast was intrinsically talented, but I had to find a way to focus that talent and make a show. I began to use my La MaMa and world theater training, adapting the exercises we'd done in ensembles. I made them less abstract and added improvised exercises to address the darkness and humor of a runaway's story. I started by using circle exercises to audition ten to twenty-five kids at a time—exercises similar to the ones in this book. These are always exercises done in a circle, where all are equal and no one is on the line.

But first let me tell you how I found my cast. It wasn't in a studio with mirrors. I hung out in various locations where I might find kids who'd want to participate in a show. I walked the Lower East Side of New York, where a program for Nuyorican—short for New York Puerto Rican—poets had a fabulous, beat-up outdoor theater with weeds growing between the seats. They employed and mentored runaways as well as kids who'd gotten out of prison and latchkey children. For a while I had an ex–gang leader who was my guide, and it was from his world that I hired an ex-junkie with sad, shiny eyes. He could tell stories and try to act frightening, although he wasn't. I also sat in Washington Square Park and watched the skateboarders doing their tricks. I found one masterful skateboarder-dancer who had me follow him in a game of cat and mouse; it turned out that he was homeless and a self-taught martial artist. I found myself in an attic that housed a small community center above a chicken coop in the Bronx. I found a towheaded fourteen-year-old boy of Italian heritage whose Bronx accent was so thick I could hardly understand him, but he showed me a combination of courage and sweetness I couldn't resist. I visited churches and visited a "special" school—I guess it was a place for "the learning-impaired" or just plain troublemakers. I found a ten-year-old hippie kid who played the violin—badly. I hired a graffiti artist and a teenage father. I also held auditions at Joseph Papp's theater and invited the "professional children" who had agents and managers. (I still don't know what a professional child is.) I didn't want to exclude any races, religions, or economic backgrounds. And, of course, I asked several of my friends to join the company.

What were the circle auditions? I realized that the usual auditions for a musical—sing eight bars of a song and read a bit of dialogue—would tell me nothing I needed to know. I'd never figure out who would be right for my show in that amount of time. I didn't want to scare my potential "actors" or myself to death. So I gathered the kids together, as I've said, and began doing the exercises and improvs that are in this book. Some of the exercises came from the international groups I had worked with and observed; some I improvised on the spot. Risk and danger can be inspiring, and at that time they really got my adrenaline going. There were moments when my mind faded to white and fifteen people stood there looking at me as if I were an insane person who liked to put people in circles. I discovered that as the leader I had to be as energetic and concentrated as I wanted my potential "actors" to be. In other words, I had to be very entertaining. Since then, I've never forgotten that an audition is a fifty-fifty proposition. You're not a judge giving out verdicts, because the auditions come right back at you. Are you and your ideas worth the trouble? Are you the kind of person somebody wants to spend hours with every day? As a leader, this mutuality becomes essential. The whole process is one of give-and-take. (I'll discuss this further in Chapter 1.)

My final cast numbered twenty-three or twenty-five (I've lost count—people came and went). They were a stunningly diverse group of young people who, in many instances, didn't have a clue why they were there; most of them had never seen a play before. Their notion of music was tapes and radio. They knew acting from TV and movies. Somehow I realized that explaining theater would be a disaster. What would I say? You get on a stage and you . . . sometimes you don't even get on a stage! So I continued with exercises, games, improvs, and storytelling; I let myself and the cast learn as we went. The theme was running away—from home, from a boyfriend or girlfriend, from a predator, from the police, from the social welfare system, from the pressures of school, from the expectations of others, from your fears, and, most of all, from yourself. We all agreed on that premise.

It took half a year to put the show together. Little by little we built a world where runaways came together, told their stories, and acted out the hardships they'd endured. We also spoke of the ways we'd all survived, and the dreams we continued to carry with us, if only our lives would work out. Some days we were articulate but undisciplined; other days, the reverse was true. At first I was terrified by the inconsistency, but after a month or two I grew to expect it and worked with moods and even temporary disappearances. During the process, we built up our bodies, strengthened our voices, and talked to one another in different ways—through song, monologues, puppets and props, signs, verbal and nonverbal dialogue, movement and dance. We created live pictures. We ate lunch and talked about nothing. We got involved with the news. We found that many runaways had similar reasons for taking off, and even if the reasons were not always the same, we found that we often shared many of the same deep and conflicted emotions.

When I worked with the group on *Runaways*, I felt I was using all my training and experience, I was pushing myself past any work I'd done before. As time passed, my writing and composition, which I'd started alone, became influenced by the language, stories, and characters of the group. The actors contributed to the direction and dances. We imagined our experiences in the streets, in shelters, in special schools, in torn-apart households, with ambitious parents, neglectful parents, or parents who lied and kept secrets. The show also spoke about the pain of leaving home as well as about the wish to have a safe and loving place to call home. Perhaps rehearsal became home for some of us. We also did parodies of ourselves—for instance, the poor, forlorn teenager. We tried very hard to stay away from clichés and from simply giving a morose message. We wanted to speak from the gut, but with skill and control. When the cast finally performed, the audience could feel their pride, their ownership of the piece, and each individual's confidence, and this added a special magic to the show. *Runaways* made it all the way to Broadway and showed American kids that theater could be young and personal. After that success, I decided to devote much of my career to creating pieces and possibilities for kids in theater. I knew it was a healing art—one that I believe all kinds of young people can benefit from doing. But they've had no exposure, and probably don't even know it's there.

I've been very lucky in my theater life and with music and writing; it's been rich and full. And I think a great deal of my energy comes from uniting theater with adolescents and children. For instance, I remember that during a tour of Africa, I learned how the spirit of young people can inspire a whole crowd. At that time I was the youngest, so each time we entered a village, I was told to take out my twelve-string guitar and start strumming. Soon children would arrive to see what this strange white girl was up to. I'd start singing to them—singing made-up songs with made-up syllables. At first they'd think I was an insane person and feel a little sorry for me. Then they'd giggle and shout at one another to try to figure out what to do. Eventually they'd start answering back, imitating me and making sounds of their own. And after a while we'd jell and sing a funny, wild-sounding chorus as more and more children added on. It was like a goofy cheering crowd in a football stadium of little children—a stadium full of singing little children. Then the parents and relatives would join the group to see why their children were making so much noise. And then young men would bring drums. By then the adult actors had a full audience, and they'd lay out a carpet on which they'd stage their show. I remember the wide range of sounds the children and I traded back and forth. I vibrated with their voices; the emotions we shared lived in the sounds and in their faces. I felt spontaneous and free, for I was immersed in waves of excitement and curiosity. And at times the noise became an African, American, Jewish, Catholic, urban rhythm-and-blues gospel choir. Surprising and beautiful!

I thought to myself that if this energy, innocence, and gorgeous noise could be organized into a unique kind of theater, we'd end up with a youthful theater in which we'd see life from a new perspective. A new energy. This is one of the many gifts that evolved from my training and apprenticeships. Thirty years later, these ideas still hold true. For me, theater is not just entertainment. Theater is discovery and adventure. It's challenging what's acceptable while you create new stories. It's celebrating what is clear and true. It's laughing and creating laughter. It can make people cry, too. Through theater, you can lead your audience into different kinds of thought. You might encourage love or provoke an argument. Who knows? You learn that the world is huge and full of pain and possibility. You are not the center of the universe, but neither are you alone. Theater can open up your life and help spring you free. Performers and creators are human beings calling out to one another and to whatever spirits or gods they believe exist. They are up there on that stage helping audiences forget their daily woes. Theater is here and now. It's live. You take in life and spit it out again in the form of a show to an audience of hopeful people. You are able to give a part of yourself to others and feel them give back to you. It takes hard work to accomplish this kind of real magic, but every step along the way has been worth it to me.

When I work in a school, I find that the classroom becomes transformed into a whole new place; a place of freedom and imagination. Theater can create a wonderful alchemy in which an auditorium becomes the home of fantasy and rants alike. The teacher becomes transformed from a disciplinarian to the leader of an adventure with words, music, and movement. Often, it is the theater teacher in a high school who gives students courage and inspires them to attempt to find a career in the arts.

On the other hand, working in the theater doesn't always have to be profound—you can have a great time just showing off. You can pick up a funny hat, try a voice, chance a step, or play an air guitar. You can put yourself in Antarctica or on the beach in Bora Bora. You can be a monster or a gangster, speak in an odd accent, step behind a podium, or run for president. You can declare words of undying love to a lamppost or die a slow death in the kitchen. You can go anywhere, to any time, and imitate a friend or make up a character that doesn't exist. Toddlers make great theater because they know how to play with 100 percent of their imagination. You have to play, too, it's part of the job. In fact, most of the exercises we will do in this book are intended to get us back to the place where we play without embarrassment. We will go a long distance to become like very young children who absolutely believe in their own worlds. But this time, we will have skills, and not only for ourselves. We have stories to share.

AT PLAY

ONE

BEING THE DIRECTOR

IT'S DIFFICULT to be a director and *not* be a director at the same time. On the one hand, you want to set up a structure that keeps the work organized and safe. But the goal, in this instance, is also to impart the specific mechanics of the theater process to your students, and let them pull apart and remake technique and tradition. You want to give a sense of how arduous it is to put together a show, and at the same time make the students hungry to rewrite the rules. You want to teach specific skills while simultaneously encouraging freedom of the imagination. You must impose strict discipline while bringing forth uninhibited energy.

You, as the director, are the one who teaches the exercises, leads the discussions, and sets forth the ideas of form, theme, and content. But I've discovered from years of leading adolescent groups that you have to become a teacher who denies being a teacher and a leader who never dictates or pontificates. You have to be able to change course in a second and, like a jazz improviser, alter the direction of the work according to the student's energy and mood. In this work there are no ultimatums. Students either choose on their own to take the risk or not (and some won't choose right away, so you have to be patient).

Even if you are a teacher in a school, teaching in a classroom, it's up to you to make your students' theater experiences different from their day-to-day classes. All directors of young people have to be highly aware and energized themselves, for the role of a director is to make the actors want to participate and dig deep inside for the best of themselves. A director doesn't "make" students perform. She creates a whole atmosphere that is conducive to humor, exploration, and taking risks. She is a benign gang leader. In fact, she has to be the most intense performer of all—and then be willing to disappear.

I go on about this because a large percentage of what makes good directing is letting go of expectations. If you come into a project already knowing what a show is, who's cast in what role, what the blocking is, and what the interpretation will be, then very few of the exercises I present will be helpful to you. That style of directing involves a different kind of method and ego. The theater I am writing about requires that you believe your students have inside them the potential to make a theater of their own. You have to truly want to *listen* to them. No matter how sullen or nervous or withdrawn they are at the start, you have to know that something powerful and interesting will come out. As a director, your investment is in creating great theater, and therefore you must stay absolutely dedicated to the health and vision of your students.

So don't try to dress like a homeboy, but perhaps dress down a little for the occasion. Create an atmosphere that is comfortable and personal so your students will feel more at ease than they do in the schoolroom every day. And announce the rules right from the start so that the boundaries are clear and the work doesn't become about enforcing them. These are the rules I set up for my actors before every workshop or rehearsal period:

1. I designate a spot in the room that is "holy." That's where we'll do exercises and improvs. I make a circle within that space and

keep that circle sacred. Everywhere else should have the feel of freedom, where you can have pillows, popcorn, or posters, but that particular space and circle are not to be messed with.

2. No attitude. My message to the actors is: You mouth off to me or someone else in the group or disrespect the work and you're out.

3. I care very much about how your day-to-day lives affect you, but I won't allow moods and acting out during the workshop hours. Before and after hours, you can have all my attention and I'll do everything I can to listen to you and help you. But your job is not to bring your troubles into the circle or even the rehearsal room.

4. You will not criticize or make fun of one another's work. First of all, it's rude, and second, you don't know enough.

5. You have to trust I won't make a fool of you or myself.

6. No violence, drugs, or alcohol.

7. No romantic or sexual behavior in the room.

I think anyone who aspires to be a director or teacher must find objectivity within himself or herself that transcends habitual categorizations of young people. You can't have a personal agenda if you want to serve the show's best interests. Instead, you have to find a way to neutralize your likes and dislikes, and in that way strive to be as open and devoid of censorship as you hope your students will be. If you can achieve this level of objectivity, you'll be constantly surprised that individuals who make up your ensemble and the ensemble as a whole will grow stronger. This kind of energy creates shows and performances that work for audiences in two ways: they feel the depth of the stories and character and also unconsciously absorb the unified and committed spirit of the cast.

Think of times when you've been in a group or classroom led by an individual who was overbearing or who allowed chaos. Now think of who inspired you, and made you want the hours never to end.

Finally, I see no advantage to forcing a young actor to reach deep down into his gut, to share the unrecognized agonizing terrors and abuses of his life. I know this might seem odd, considering I often work in areas of child abuse, violence, and loss. Even so, I think unlimited personal confessions are extremely dangerous in the younger years. As theater artists and teachers, none of us are qualified to deal with the consequences of provoking a troubled child or teenager — or any child or teenager, for that matter — as he plunges into a nightmarish reliving of moments of terror or pain. It's especially tempting to turn issue-oriented theater work into bad therapy, but bad therapy makes bad theater. I believe that if you work for the good of the artist — for the quality of the show — you are actually getting deeper truths from each individual. In my rehearsals I always say, "Tell me a story about a time when something happened, it doesn't matter if it's true, just make it a good story." Or "Let me see a character who . . ." and then I advise them to create the character through the body and the voice — even if the character is the student herself.

In those rare moments when you can't help scaring or upsetting the actors, stay in control of the time you take. For instance, if I'm staging a disturbing scene with violence or death, I do it during one day and then I don't repeat the scene until some time later. Once the kids know it as a part of a whole, that's fine, but the initial staging of a dark moment, if it's good, may feel too real. When we were making my show called *The Violence Project*, we spent several hours making horrific images that required buckets of fake blood, but we also did slapstick and improvs about the fact that it was indeed fake. I balanced the horrible images with horrible humor. If we are telling upsetting stories, I allow for five or six stories and then move on to something more physical. And after we experience what might be a heartbreaking and scary day, at the end of the rehearsal I always put on loud music so everyone can dance.

After I establish the rules, I then have to get the young actors used to "being directed," which is very different from being taught. They have to hear me with not just their ears but also their bodies. They have to understand quickly and expect rapid changes.

BEGINNING EXERCISES

In the beginning, you should be the first person to demonstrate any exercise. This humanizes you and explains what the exercise is about in a precise, active way. Also, if the students see that you are willing to let loose, so will they. No exercise should ever go beyond three minutes and it usually should be completed in one and a half to two minutes. You can cut off exercises very quickly if you feel the students are losing concentration or energy. One of your jobs is to make sure time is used fully and well: long pauses will allow doubt and fear and adolescent embarrassment to get too strong a hold. After one or two sessions you can slow down the pace a tiny bit.

Don't get too serious or too oriented toward end results. Each day is an event in itself and has its ups and downs and laughter. The work can't be focused solely on putting up a show: both you and the students must enjoy the process itself. That joy and curiosity will be reflected in anything you make. Ninety percent of the time, even when working on serious material, the work should be, at its core, really fun.

First, let's start with some basic exercises. A sense of playfulness and gamesmanship, as well as openness and daring, should be present in rehearsals.

Movement Commands

Aim: To sharpen reflexes; loosen up to relieve tension; create laughter.

Exercise 1.1: The students stand in an informal group facing you. Make an opening speech, but stick in "commands" through the whole speech that the group must follow. This is a great game.

Example: "So we are at rehearsal on the first day (*sit*) and I want you (*stand*) to know how excited I (*sit*) am to have you (*stand*) here with me (*jump*) and I hope (*sit*) you can (*stand jump turn*) work with me on (*sit*) on (*spin*) your dreams (*stand jump spin sit*) because (*sit*) your (*stand*) dreams (*sit*) are (*stand*) (*sit stand sit stand sit stand*) are important to (*lie down*) me.

Exercise 1.2: Let several other students, one at a time, improvise a speech sneaking in their own commands.

Note: This is not about power. It's about waking and speeding up the students' reaction time.

Wrong Names

Aim: To work on timing; humor.

Exercise 1.3: Stand in a group spread out like guests at a cocktail party. Introduce yourselves informally by first names. Begin to slip in the names of famous people. Every time a famous person is named rather than one of you, the group has to say or make a sound that signifies "Wrong."

Example:

PERSON 1: Hi, I'm Jack.

PERSON 2: I'm Sarah.

PERSON 3: My name's David.

PERSON 4: I'm Susan.

PERSON 5: I'm Derek.

PERSON 1: I'm Leonardo DiCaprio.

GROUP: WRONNG

PERSON 1: I'm Jack.

PERSON 2: I'm Bono.

GROUP: WRONNG

PERSON 3: I'm Mickey Mouse.

GROUP: WRONNG

PERSON 4: My name's Susan.

PERSON 5: I'm the Hulk.

GROUP: WRONNG

Conducting Tatay

Aim: To heighten hearing skills and open up the imagination to sound.

Exercise 1.4: The students gather before you in an informal group. You give them the sound *Tatay*. (I choose this short rhythmic sound because it is simple and resonant and because *ta* is the first beat in East Indian music.) You act as a conductor and they repeat "Tatay" to the rhythm, speed, and dynamic with which you conduct with your hands and your own speech. At first you keep your conducting even, and then begin to change the pace more frequently.

After you have conducted, several students should try to do it.

Example:

Ta Tay Ta Tay Ta Tay Ta Tay Ta Tay Ta Tay Ta Tay

moderate_____to_____loud

Ta Tay Ta Tay Ta Tay   TaTayTaTayTaTayTaTay

moderate_____to_____fast

TATAYTATAYTATAY TaaaaaaaaTaaaaaayTaaaaaaaaaTaaaaaaay

loud and fast_____to_____moderate and held out long

TaTayTaTayTaTayTaTay   ta   tay   ta   tay   ta   tay

whispered_____to_____moderate with spaces in between

TATAYTATAYTATAY TATAYTATAYTATAY

very loud _____to_____moderate

As a result of this exercise, students will lose self-consciousness and begin to get a taste of the voice as instrument and the joy of making sounds.

Follow the Leader

Aim: To acquire awareness of the body without thinking; to learn to be instinctive.

Exercise 1.5: Lead the students around the entire space, and, if possible, out the door. Explain that each person needs to watch the person directly in front to know what style of stepping, walking, or running is coming from you.

Then let other students be the leader.

Move to Music

Aim: To learn to physically respond to different rhythms and melodies.

Exercise 1.6: Play a mix of music on a CD in vastly different styles and tell everyone in the group to move with their eyes closed.

1. Polka
2. Techno
3. Spaghetti Western music
4. Funk
5. A symphonic overture
6. Sound effects
7. Big Band
8. A poet reciting his or her verse
9. Choose your own

Everyday Activities

Aim: To learn to give up inhibitions and make dreams a physical reality. (This will help the student connect to his or her imagination, which is good for improvisation and character work. When making or acting in a piece, the student will be more in touch with what the body can do.)

Exercise 1.7: Ask each student to think about an activity he or she would do in his or her room. Have the students spread out and act out what they would do.

Example: I might say, "One of the things I like to do in my room when no one can see me is to play air guitar like a rock and roll star." I demonstrate by strumming an invisible guitar and jump with all the machismo and power I can.

MANY STUDENTS I work with have never seen a play; their idea of acting is formed by film and television. Perhaps they've studied Shakespeare, but none of his characters are as real to them as those on TV. Therefore, when students act, they consciously go straight for clichés. For them, characters are defined by stereotypes, and contemporary history is taught mostly in news programs or action adventure movies. This is not a diatribe against TV and movies; I'm as big an addict as anyone. But when directing or teaching theater, it's important to break down stereotypes and clichés so the student can recognize what's his or hers and not an easy imitation. When you do a cliché, it means you're doing a move, gesture, or characterization that's been done so much that it's almost mocking itself. A cliché and stereotype can be used to define wrongly the characteristics of a race or ethnic group. In short, it's the easy way to portray a character or emotion. Here are some examples:

1. A cowboy chewing tobacco and spitting it out
2. A blond-haired babe acting stupid and cutesy
3. A hippie being high
4. A thug being a thug
5. A Hispanic or African American being a drug dealer
6. A Jewish woman who's money hungry
7. A little child being overly sweet and excited by cereal
8. A nerdy guy with big glasses

Unfortunately, there are so many clichés that whole shows can be made of them.

Exploring Stereotypes

Aim: To identify habits learned from TV and movies. To strengthen the ability to perform in front of one another. To identify, imitate, and break down stereotypes while working on finding character and laughter.

Exercise 1.8: Ask the students to imitate the following situations and characters using clichés:

1. A detective thinking about his murder case. He suffers as he tries to figure out clues
2. A bride who discovers her new husband is a serial murderer
3. A pimp threatening his girls
4. A computer analyst with no emotions
5. A drug dealer denying he's a drug dealer
6. A teenage hooker trying to pick up a trick
7. A scientific nerd trying to discuss a new discovery
8. A soldier who's been driven mad by war
9. A tough, shrewish wife
10. A rock star singing his greatest hit
11. A softhearted Mafia lieutenant
12. A female CIA agent

Exercise 1.9: Discuss the phoniness of these characters. Though they are fun to play, they're not real. The mannerisms and voices the students display are often copies of what they've picked up from the media. Try to figure out the source of their characterizations.

Exercise 1.10: Now try national, religious, racial, sexual, and age stereotypes:

1. Arabic/African/Pakistani/Indian/ex-hippie taxi drivers
2. A hip-hop artist
3. A dumb farmer

4. A hillbilly

5. An overly sexy woman

6. Puerto Rican/Asian/Italian/African American/skinhead/Goth gang members

7. A "retard"

8. A jock

9. A biker

10. A Jewish mother/father/grandfather

11. A Hasidic Jew

12. A black kid being tough

13. White/Jewish/African American/Puerto Rican teenage girls

14. An Asian deli owner

15. An Asian honor student

16. A Puerto Rican dancing to a boom box

Exercise 1.11: Now try the most serious stereotypes:

1. The rich and cheap Jew

2. The African American street thug

3. The lazy Puerto Rican

4. The Chinese waiter screaming in a restaurant

5. The goody-goody white girl

6. White trash

These are more than simple acting exercises, as they reveal long-held ideas we have about one another. If you keep it *comic*, no one will be offended, and it can, in fact, be quite liberating. I strongly suggest that in the beginning, each student make fun of a person of his or her own race or religion to avoid creating unnecessary tensions.

Emotional Stereotypes

Aim: To identify false emotions and learn to exude confidence in performance; create laughter.

Exercise 1.12: Now try exploring more complicated instances in which the expression of a moment or state of being becomes a cliché, going over the top until the emotion is twisted or damaged.

1. A sorrowful woman crying on Oprah (or in an interview on the news)
2. A jaw-grinding, tough cop all bent up inside, demanding justice for his partner
3. A fearful person watching an earthquake that is bringing the San Francisco–Oakland Bay Bridge down
4. A girl madly in love
5. An angry Russian spy
6. A lustful Transylvanian vampire
7. A crazy bum totally out of it, drunk and begging
8. A person in terror of going mad
9. A person feeling the pain of having a heart attack
10. A person feeling the relief of getting away from someone who's chasing him or her
11. An athlete feeling pride in having won a great game
12. An actor accepting an Academy Award
13. An angry, threatening person who's been betrayed
14. A person dying violently because of stabbing/shooting/poison
15. A person dying slowly and revealing lost, deeply secret facts
16. A person facing death in a strong way, telling the living to go on

17. A person sadly fading out

18. A soldier bravely dying for his buddies in a war

Later on, some of these states of being can be worked with seriously, but try to keep the tone light until we get to the technical exercises.

THERE WAS A Russian poet named Osip Mandelstam who used to hum to himself—sometimes for days—until the hum became words. At that certain point he knew his poem was ready to be written. I have a friend who's an actress-songwriter who goes to the park and throws balls for her Portuguese water dog. This back-and-forth, back-and-forth, is the constant beat that becomes the internal rhythm for a new song. I know a choreographer who has watched a flock of ostriches at the zoo and, in her imagination, turned them into a group of dancers who rush maniacally about while jerking their heads in a comic dance.

For myself, I tell my students that I lie on my couch, half asleep, and imagine whole plays. Sometimes I'm in them; sometimes I'm directing them. I see the stage. The lights. A character sitting on a chair or hiding behind a curtain. What is he saying? What will he do next? We can dream about the images that haunt us—nightmares, the news, our little fights, our loneliness or acts of cruelty, even death. I explain that we can try to use these dark dreams to fill our stage. We can expose our fears, or speak out against injustices. But we can see ourselves falling in love. We can touch a mysterious lover on the cheek, dance with him, or pull a chair out from under him (depending on the kind of love). We might build a model airplane and believe we are one of the Wright brothers or sit by an imaginary riverbank like Huckleberry Finn. We can experience different moods, desires, language, and physical circumstances as our dreams become more specific. We can imagine the impulses we share with other individuals, whether they resemble us or come from a whole different background or era.

Dreaming

Aim: To learn visualization and open imagination.

Exercise 1.13:

1. Early on, encourage your students to visualize and dream about what character they want to be, what world they want to inhabit, and what will happen in their world. Dreaming helps creativity and helps students to understand metaphor.

2. If your students aren't inclined toward dreaming and even scoff at it, have them close their eyes and experiment. Start wide with broad landscapes, cities, or big feelings, such as a jealous rage or the thrill of a great sports win. Tell them to settle on a specific location, whether it is a mountaintop or a kitchen table. Ask them:
   a. Who's there?
   b. What are they doing?

3. Ask them now to imagine their creation as a play.
   a. Is it on a stage?
   b. What kind of stage?

Tell them that a stage is somewhere where an audience can join you as your dreams turn into a real piece of theater. It can be inside or outside on a roof or a stadium or a rock hall. It can be a backyard. Ask your students if they see such a place, inhabited by characters who are living made-up lives. If they can dream theater, they probably can create it.

PETER BROOK

During the early days when I was working at La MaMa, I was lucky enough to be asked to join a special theater ensemble led by a renowned director named Peter Brook. Brook is a British director who, having done extraordinary versions of Shakespeare and other classics, decided in the 1960s that it was time he explored the possibilities of a new kind of theater. He wrote a book called *The Empty Space* that is a bible for many theater artists.

Peter was fascinated by the dances, dramas, and rituals of other cultures. He studied and witnessed many ancient and contemporary third-world traditions. You might want to search for some photographs of the cultures he explored because you'll see colors, costumes, and places that can stretch your imagination. Later on, if you have the opportunity you might be inspired to travel to some of these countries. Here is a list of just some of Peter Brook's inspirations:

West African storytelling and dance

Hindu legends and Kathakali dancing

Japanese acting and the Noh and Kabuki theater

Arabic legends

Kabbalistic studies

Indonesian dancing and shadow puppets

Trance dancing of voodoo

Persian drumming and extinct Persian languages

Turkish and Sufi spinning

Gypsy lore

Secret customs and ceremonies of many East Asian and Middle
   Eastern religions

Another reason for researching these cultures is that you'll be surprised how many of the forms and ideas have influenced modern American culture (everything from New Age music to hip-hop comes from somewhere else). Peter Brook was hungry for adventure. He traveled all over, devoured information, and then used what he saw by integrating it into his own theater pieces.

He formed a theater company made up of actors, performers, and creators from all over the world. The company was based in Paris, and I joined them after they'd been together for three years. Peter saw a piece of my work and invited me to compose for him. Ellen Stewart told me I should stay in Paris, where he worked, and have an adventure. I had no idea what I was getting myself into. For all I knew, Peter Brook could've been a guru with a Mercedes and a mansion outside of Beverly Hills; I didn't have any idea that he was a visionary director. On my "Mama's" advice, I gave up everything and went to live in Paris. At the age of twenty it seemed important to take risks. I was especially interested in a trip to Africa that Brook's company was going to take, and if I made it through the Paris months, I would get to go. As it turned out, the exercises and techniques I use have their origins in my travels with that group. La MaMa and Peter Brook changed my way of thinking about theater.

The members of Peter Brook's international company were all quite different from one another. The group consisted of a dancer from Mali, a Noh actor from Japan, a black German cabaret singer, a Jewish Brit, several members of the Royal Shakespeare Company of London, two avant-garde American actors, and a Middle Eastern/French television star. Later on he'd add many more nationalities with even more diverse backgrounds. English and French were the two languages the group depended on, but few of the French knew English and the Americans hardly knew French; the African understood French, but talked in English; the Japanese actor barely understood English *or* French; and early on we began acting out phrases with elaborate hand gestures and body language, even if the person to whom we were talking was from the same country and understood every word.

Outside rehearsals, we went our different ways, in different groups. We had separate tastes in foods, different opinions on politics, music, and even about what was important for the theater. We fell in love with one another and had passionate disagreements; we dressed differently and laughed at different jokes. What one person found beautiful, another might find hideous. What one found brilliant and inspiring, another found boring and dumb. Our different cultures made us fascinating and confusing to one another, and at times caused difficult misunderstandings.

There was one place, however, where all attitudes and superficial thinking were set aside: the carpet. We came together around a square carpet that was laid out on the cement floor. In Peter Brook's company, when you gathered around the carpet, you had to be ready to concentrate and work; nothing from the outside was allowed to be brought inside. This is what influenced me in my use of the circle. At first, Peter Brook imposed the sanctity of the carpet on his actors, but after a while each individual began to feel a sense of protectiveness for the quiet and concentrated time that the carpet represented. Hilarious improvs, dances, hideous creatures, and frightening slapstick scenes could explode on the carpet. You could be gross, outrageous, scatological, or as dark and dangerous as you dared to go. You could be lyrical and mysterious. You might find a tender moment, or a joyous sound. The carpet was the place where you abandoned yourself and used your voice, body, and imagination to explore the unknown. It was a safe place, so that it was there that you could take your greatest risks. Flop your greatest flops. Squeak your loudest squeaks. Jump high. Crawl.

In the same way, I use the circle as a place where actors can learn to become an ensemble. Many theater companies and college instructors use a circle for exercises. Everyone can see everyone else and in a circle each individual is equal. You don't put on shows for one another or try to compete; instead, you become one another's most devoted audience.

CREATING AN ENSEMBLE

The following are a group of exercises that should be started early and used throughout the whole process. They will help individual students form an ensemble, since they will help them see and hear and sense one another with more sensitivity and awareness, as well as help them learn appreciation for silence. The students will start to understand how to pick up on the inner music of theater and how transitions from one active moment to another are as essential as the scenes themselves. Besides that, these exercises are playful and challenging. Theater should be like sports, requiring intense activity. It should also encourage originality and help develop the skills we need to draw in a greater diversity of students to the theater.

Exercises 1.14–1.31 should be performed in a standing circle and supervised by the director. Often they will involve a beat. The director keeps the beat, watches the exercise, and, if it gets fouled up, decides to start over or move on to another one. Never let the circle deteriorate into chaos; chaos is exhausting and confusing.

I prefer to keep things going at a good clip and rarely allow long discussions. Actors should never criticize or direct one another, so there's not much to say. My rhythm may end up being different from what you need, but it's essential to keep the element of play in the exercises, like a basketball game. And don't forget novelty. And humor.

Tennis Ball

Aim: To learn timing, awareness, and how to work together.

Exercise 1.14: Pass a tennis ball around the circle exactly on a beat. Keep going on the even beat until the company has reached a fluid rhythm. This may take time. After accomplishing the art of passing and taking one ball, you can start to add complications. Speed up the beat. Add another tennis ball. Add more complications without losing the beat. Reverse the direction. Stand on one leg. See how many balls the circle can keep going at the same time without losing the beat and without dropping the ball. Get as complicated as is comfortable and energizing for the group. Try passing the ball while you jump and say "Chile con carne" at the same time.

Aim: To learn names and to work on awareness.

Exercise 1.15: One person should say the name of someone in the circle and simultaneously throw the tennis ball toward him or her. The receiver should call the name of another and throw the ball to him or her. After the actors get used to the exercise, add a tennis ball so two actors will be throwing and calling names simultaneously. Use as many balls at a time as is possible without catastrophe and midair collision.

Aim: To learn to respond to quick changes.

Exercise 1.16: Call the name of one person and throw the ball to the person to his or her left or right. Then, call the name of one person and throw it to any other person in the circle.

Aim: To open up imagination; to get the members of the group to enjoy one another.

Exercise 1.17: Pass the tennis ball around and have each actor quickly make it into something else, such as a telephone, a baby, a potato to eat, an alien creature.

Aim: To explore expressing emotion without words.

Exercise 1.18: Pass the tennis ball to the next person with a specific emotion—fear, love, sneakiness, anger, and so on. The interpretation of the emotion should be expressed in the whole body and especially the hands. Try to keep away from "mugging." Using faces often detracts from the dramatic expression of the body as a *whole*.

Rhythmic Patterns

Aim: To work with rhythm; learn names.

Exercise 1.19: Pass a clap around the circle. Have each student take the energy of the person before and pass it to the next. The clap should get faster and louder, slower and softer.

Exercise 1.20: One person clapping or playing a drum provides a steady beat. Going around the circle, each person says, "My name is . . ." followed by his or her name said out loud to the beat. The object is to stay with the beat, get to know it, and learn how the rhythms of the names go against it.

Aim: To get to know one another; rhythm; quicken instincts and ensemble skill.

Exercise 1.21: Going around the circle, have each person say, "My name is . . ." followed by the name and one simple personal fact. For example, "My name is Liz Swados and I'm wearing blue sneaks." Everyone must speak in rhythm.

Next, go around the circle in the opposite direction; say your name and a different personal fact. For example, "My name is Liz Swados and I have a poodle named Billy Bob."

Aim: To learn more about being in formation as a group and to vary rhythm.

Exercise 1.22: Go around the circle several times using "My name is . . ." and different facts. Notice how words fit onto and in between the beats. Try not to repeat the feeling of the person next to you; rhythmic patterns can be unconsciously contagious.

Aim: To learn the rhythm of conversation and to focus.

Exercise 1.23: Now begin an easy conversation, keeping the words and sentences going against the beat. This is not unlike rap, but it shouldn't rhyme and should stay casual and hooked into the moment. Keep the conversation simple: the weather, what you ate for breakfast. Stop the exercise if actors go too much off the beat or substitute conversation for good rhythm.

Example:

PERSON 1: (*on the beat*) What a nice T-shirt you're wearing.

PERSON 2: (*on the beat*) Thank you very, very much.

Aim: To learn to use music and movement and to gather confidence by teaching coordination of mind and body.

Exercise 1.24: One person stamps, claps, and snaps to form a simple rhythmic pattern; don't use words. The rest of the group imitates. Each member of the circle offers a variation on stamping, clapping, and snapping, with the group imitating.

Example:

PERSON 1: *snap, snap, stamp, clap*

GROUP: *snap, snap, stamp, clap*

The second person does a different pattern and the group imitates.

PERSON 2: *snap, stamp, snap, stamp, clap*

GROUP: *snap, stamp, snap, stamp, clap*

Aim: To learn to use sound and movement to gain further confidence, coordination of mind and body, memory.

Exercise **1.25:** The first student offers a combination of claps, snaps, and stamps. The group imitates. The next person repeats that first pattern and then adds on one of his or her own, creating a sequence that contains both patterns. This goes around the circle until each person and the group as a whole has to remember a very long sequence of rhythmic patterns. If someone messes up—can't remember—the group should assist that person.

Example:

PERSON 1: *snap, snap, stamp, clap*

GROUP: *snap, snap, stamp, clap*

PERSON 2: *snap, snap, stamp, clap, stamp, clap, stamp, clap*

GROUP: *snap, snap, stamp, clap, stamp, clap, stamp, clap*

This is much like the game "I'm going to the country, and I'm going to bring—a picnic basket; I'm going to the country, and I'm going to bring—a picnic basket and a pair of roller skates; I'm going to the country, and I'm going to bring—a picnic basket, a pair of roller skates, and the president of the United States . . . ," but without words, in rhythm, to a beat.

REASON FOR THE BEAT

When I was in Africa, I noticed that the first sounds you heard in any show or ceremony were the drums. I traveled alongside an Uraba drummer from Nigeria named Ian Sola, who hopped on one leg, played his "talking drum," and drove the actors into wild dances and improvisations off of his rhythmic patterns. He rarely talked in any language and stole my candy bars and batteries whenever he could, but his playing gave the group enormous energy. When I searched the Lower East Side of New York looking for runaway kids for my show *Runaways*, I ran into a group of Latino drummers who talked to each other with different patterns of hitting a conga drum, scraping nails on the drumhead, and striking garbage cans, bells, guerros, and claves. It occurred to me that voices could be drums talking to one another with and without words. The driving force of a beat creates a sense of urgency and cohesiveness that wouldn't exist otherwise. A beat keeps a group together in the beginning when they have no other reason or skills to join and merge; a beat is a shared experience that resonates within the body. We will use the beat often in our exercises, and when we stop, we will still feel the presence of a strong tempo.

Many Parts

Aim: To heighten awareness and skills of observation.

Exercise 1.26: One student mentions a place or object that requires many parts. The rest of the company fills in the parts.

Example:

PERSON 1: a bicycle

PERSON 2: handlebars

PERSON 3: wheels

PERSON 4: chain

PERSON 5: pedals

PERSON 6: brakes

(and so on)

Other examples:

1. park
2. tool box
3. baby's room
4. trunk of a car

Bamboo Sticks

Aim: To create a relationship between the body and simple expression and movement. To work on group concentration and coordination.

Exercise 1.27:

1. Gather a group of poles or bamboo sticks of equal length, no longer than five feet. Look at the sticks as if they are extensions of the body. Are they alive with energy? Students in a standing circle should touch the floor in the center with their sticks—one stick per actor. They should lift the ends of the sticks up simultaneously, not trying to be faster or slower, just absolutely in sync.
2. Hold each stick like a baseball bat at the waist. Everyone should lift the sticks over their heads simultaneously.
3. Have each person make the stick something else and demonstrate to the ensemble, who imitate. For example: an oar, a long spoon, stirring a pot, a horn.

4. Stand in a circle with the stick at waist height, each student's stick touching another at the end. Move sideways, but keep the stick circle still.

5. Pass the sticks around, keeping them vertical. The sticks should stay perfectly upright and not waver. Now try this to a beat.

6. Start with the stick ends on the floor in the middle; hold them diagonally as if you're reaching out with a hoe. Now lift the sticks together. Lower them.

7. Create a carousel with the sticks. In a circle, touch the ends in the middle and hold them diagonally (as you would a hoe) as the students move in a circle at the same pace.

8. Make the same carousel formation with the sticks and have every student make a slow up or down movement like a horse on a carousel.

9. Leaving lots of room, hold the sticks over the head as high as possible. Each student should whirl slowly and then faster, feeling one another's tempo and energy.

10. Have a limbo contest.

Put the sticks away and move on to another exercise. The group will feel in tune and more aware of what's around them.

Problem Solving

Aim: To make the group solve a problem together.

Exercise 1.28:

1. The group stands in a circle and holds hands. Keeping hands together, have one section of the group go under the arms of another section of the group (as in the game of London Bridge but

with hands held together). Students should go under one another's arms until the entire company is knotted up and can't move.

2. Breathe.

3. Now, *without letting go*, the group should slowly and carefully untangle itself.

With Drummer

Aim: To develop focus, rhythm, and listening skills.

Exercise 1.29: If possible, have a drummer join rehearsal. He or she will play rhythmic patterns on the drum and the students will reproduce the patterns as they move—the ups and downs, syncopations, louds and softs. Then reverse the sequence.

Aim: To hear rhythms inside and gain confidence to express them. To learn the theatricality of rhythm.

Exercise 1.30: Have a student move in rhythm to a drummer. If the student is feeling more comfortable, he or she can advance to "cut fours," which means the drummer does four beats and the student answers in four beats in a continuously rhythmical piece of music.

Aim: With more than one drum, learn how to feel and hear rhythm in the whole body; focus.

Exercise 1.31: One student moves in a rhythmic pattern to one drum and another student moves with a second drummer. Then repeat this and reverse direction. A variation from Africa is for one student to "drum" on another actor's head and the other to answer back the same rhythm in syllables. Try using all parts of the body as a drum.

Move while you hit, clap, and stamp. Make a rhythmic pattern that the drums (or another student) repeat.

Cultural Sounds

Aim: To expand the vocabulary of sounds, emotions, and rhythms.

Exercise 1.32: Each student in the group should be encouraged to find a recording from another culture, in another language, and to introduce it. Each should describe why he or she likes it.

Example: Michael brings in a track of Pygmy singing from Uganda.

1. The group listens.
2. MICHAEL: They sound like a carousel and like angels or those little kids who scream too much and have hoarse voices.

Here are some suggestions for your students if they don't know where to begin.

1. South African "click" singing and talking
2. Balinese gamelan and chanting (the monkey chorus)
3. Indian raga singing
4. Native American songs, drums, and flutes
5. Aboriginal chants and didgeridoo
6. Georgian Russian chorale music
7. Tibetan Buddhist chanting
8. Irish songs for the sea
9. Old English ballads
10. West Indian carnival music
11. French troubadour songs

12. Spanish tango

13. Brazilian samba and drumming

14. Klezmer music

These are examples of the vast choices open to the student. World music is now recorded on many CD labels.

Field Trip

Aim: To bring the group closer together; to develop focus and observation skills.

Exercise 1.33: Change your setting. Take a trip that is related to the theme on which your group is working.

Examples:

1. Liz is doing a show on immigration. The students visit Ellis Island.

2. Sam and his group are working on a show about baseball.
   a. Go to a game.
   b. Go to a practice.
   c. Go to the local museum that has memorabilia from the town's favorite players.

3. Lilly's group is working on a show about pressure.
   a. Go to the stock exchange.
   b. Go to a trader's office.
   c. Attend a class designed to improve SAT scores.
   d. Make a visit to a factory.

SEATED CIRCLE EXERCISES

These exercises provide a way for the members of the group to get to know one another better as well as helping them go deeper into themselves. They will help you develop your powers of observation. If the students learn to see themselves through one another's eyes, their ability to express themselves will grow. After standing and doing exercises for a long time, sitting will feel good, but concentration and focus shouldn't be lost. Some of these exercises might involve assigning "homework" one day and bringing it in the next. Students often have to do research, make observations, think about their characters, and analyze their scripts in between rehearsals. Later on, the seated circle will become the base for almost all character and writing exercises.

Object Descriptions

Aim: To introduce metaphor; to learn more about one another.

Exercise 1.34: Have each student bring an object from home that is especially precious to him or her. Go around the circle and have them show the object and explain why he or she treasures it.

Example: I might introduce my guitar to the group. I would tell them that it was handmade in Spain and I've had it for thirty years. I'd point out the cracks in the wood that came from pounding it like an electric guitar and I might say I love it because it has traveled all over the world with me and was there when I wrote all my early songs. I might say to students, "You could show a locket that has your grandmother's picture inside. Then you could talk a bit about your grandmother, why she was important to you, and how you feel her spirit in the locket. You could bring in a hairbrush and describe how good it feels when you pull this particular brush through your hair. You could show a rock your brother picked up in the desert, the first battered shoe your dog chewed on as a puppy, a wrapper from a double cheeseburger you ate on your first date."

The exercise can be tender, serious, humorous, or goofy. It introduces your superstitions and memories and starts you talking in front of one another. You begin to understand that an object can be a metaphor for a whole experience—something that brings up the feeling or sense of a moment without your having to describe the moment in a full story. You are experimenting with the idea that objects have their own lives. You are also beginning to learn how to talk concisely, to the point.

Physical Greeting

Aim: To encourage awareness and acceptance of one another.

Exercise 1.35: Go around the seated circle and have each person greet the whole group without speaking. Within this greeting, you want to express how you feel about the group. Use only the upper part of your body—your arms and hands—trying not to use your face to get your feelings across. Use the energy from your whole body.

Then go around again. Students can imitate each other's greetings and in this way learn new kinds of movement and a sense of the other person's emotional intention.

Example: I might open my arms wide and then sweep them in—a gesture of welcoming the group to my heart. I might wave one hand and turn my head, meaning "I want to be here but I'm shy." I might point a finger at various members of the group, lower my chin, and do a tough gesture, meaning "You c'mere."

Try to make the gesture clean and simple so that your movements are as precise as in a dance or sport and your energy is fully focused on making the movement. Try to make the rest of yourself stay still; let your concentration focus on the movement and the feeling you want to express through that movement.

Discuss News

Aim: To expand awareness and knowledge of what is "dramatic."

Exercise 1.36: Discuss the news. You can plan to work on any theme or story for the play you want to adapt or make. Or just talk about ideas from the news that interest you; it's important to be aware of what's going on in the world. Each day one or two students should bring in a newsworthy political or cultural story that he or she will read out loud or summarize. This is important to any ensemble because it broadens its information about human behavior. The student also gets practice in telling a story to an audience. Unfamiliar stories that are true or said to be true evoke new emotions and put personal troubles and obsessions in perspective. The student will also identify with some of the characters in the story and find new empathy for situations once taken for granted. He or she will find that stories and characters in the news will mirror themes that come up as work on the show develops in improvs, or monologues, or movement sequences.

Children's Stories

Aim: To acquire awareness of who and what makes a story. And to begin performing!

Exercise 1.37: Each student brings in a children's story to re-create for the rest of the ensemble. Each one chooses a tale that already exists but finds a new way to tell it. He or she can play around with the presentation by asking others in the group to act it out, by redoing it in rhyme or rhythm, by trying many voices, or by using signs. The story shouldn't go on very long; the student has to keep clarity and focus. But this should be an exciting adaptation of a story the student has always adored or happened to find while doing research. The student begins to develop a sense of personal taste—of what appeals to him or her and why.

In this exercise, the job of the storyteller is to relate the plot coherently without reading the writer's work word for word. The "audience" should be able to feel the suspense and identify with the emotions that the story is meant to provoke. There's a child in everyone, and the story should play to that child without becoming simplistic or a parody of itself. The more the members of the ensemble get used to performing in different genres, the more ready they'll be for an audience. They will learn about a wide variety of literature and see and hear the individual voices and characters. Understanding the range of stories and styles will open students up for trying new things. You have to be flexible in creating theater, and brave enough to take risks.

Storytelling

Aim: To heighten memory and to instill a sense of group dynamics.

Exercise 1.38: An old game: you're sitting in the circle and one of you starts a story. At a certain point—hopefully at the most unexpected moment—the person telling the story turns abruptly to the person next to him or her, who in turn has to pick up the story immediately—without hesitation—and continue on.

Example:

PERSON 1: I woke up this morning, looked in the mirror and saw—I had two noses! I thought about where I'd picked up that extra nose and then I remembered. It was at the—

PERSON 2: —circus. Yes, the circus! I was hanging out with a
     bunch of clowns and they had been passing noses around until
     we were interrupted by—

PERSON 3: —until we were interrupted by a huge hailstorm . . .
     (and so on)

Even if the story gets more and more bizarre, you hold on and
keep going with absolute authority. Authority means you express
yourself in a way that is in control and without showing any hesitation or doubt. When you have authority onstage, you look as if you
were meant to be there. Sometimes you might have to fake having
authority, and often through doing this you'll convince yourself of
your own inner strength. As Oscar Hammerstein wrote in his song "I
Whistle A Happy Tune" from *The King and I*, "For when I fool the
people I fear / I fool myself as well."

Telling Lies

Aim: To assist in acquiring "authority."

Exercise 1.39: Go around the seated circle and tell the most outrageous lie you can think of. Tell it as if it's absolutely true.

Example: I am the second cousin of Justin Timberlake. My mother
is part koala bear.

TWO

VOICE

SHAWN: Lust.

TERESINA: (*swinging her hips*) Oh, look at you baby. Oh honey baby would you look at you baby honey doll face sweet thing. Mmm Mmm Mmm. I love your ooh la la and I just gotta oh honeybaby sweet heart doll face precious dove gotta have your oohla la oomp pa pa ka zow. What I wouldn't give to have a little bit of your zaka zaka boom boom yikes eee yow bam bam hubba hubba.*

> —Shawn and Teresina, age thirteen, in *The Red Sneaks*,
> performed in 1989 for the Theater for New Audience
> (New York: Samuel French, 1991)

In the musical *Gypsy*, Mama Rose stands in the back of the theater and screeches, "SING OUT, LOUISE!" to her poor humiliated daughter. How many times have you stood in the back of the room and shouted, "Louder" or "Enunciate" or "Open your mouth, I can't under-

---

*I use quotes from different plays I've done with students to show examples of student work and to illuminate my points.

stand a word"? Most students cringe when they hear a singer going up and down a scale. They think of a stuffy classroom with a voice teacher squinting her eyes and saying, "Horrible. Do it again! Again! Again!" Some have no concept of scales at all. They have nightmares about singing in a chorus and being asked politely *not* to sing because they aren't on the same notes as everyone else. I tell them to listen more and sing less, but add, "It's not that what you're doing isn't *interesting*, but it's different." I personally believe that someone grunting with intuition can be more moving than an empty sweet voice. (The composer Charles Ives invested a similar sensibility in his music.) Working on the voice can be terrifying; it's not some instrument students can pick up and put down. It comes from inside and reveals bare naked insides. That's why students sometimes hide their voices and become purposely "stupid" when it's time to sing. I have worked with so many students who are experts at hiding their voices that I know many ways of doing it. Here are some of them:

1. Mumble
2. Talk with teeth clenched
3. Hardly move lips
4. Put a hand in front of the mouth when talking
5. Stretch neck up, down, or away from listeners when talking
6. Jiggle up and down and shake hands while talking
7. Drop the ends of sentences
8. Squeak, whine, growl
9. Eat or drink while talking
10. Look down at shoes while speaking
11. Speak words so quickly that no one can follow
12. Take so many pauses that the listener loses attention and moves on

If you want to perform, you have to deal with your voice. Actually, vocal sounds can be very liberating. You run into trouble because you think you can't sing like Aretha Franklin or fill a room without a microphone. And studying the anatomy of the throat and being told about diaphragmatic breathing provokes anxiety because you can't translate the organs circled in red to your own physical body.

Students get scared of using their voices because they believe they have to *make* a great sound. They think they have to *make* themselves understood. They have to *make* their voices travel over space. So they push and sweat and try to *make* their voices sound loud and expressive. Or beautiful. Or frightening. This kind of thinking produces odd sounds and hoarse voices.

I personally think that good sounds are made by good listening. I start off saying, "How well do you really listen? Forget about the voice right now. Just use your ears."

KALIANA KHRISHNA BAHVAKTAVAR

When I was in college, I commuted from Bennington College in Vermont to Wesleyan University in Connecticut so I could study Carnatic (South Indian) singing with a master. Carnatic singing is the classical music of southern India, and it sounds like nothing else. The rhythms are syncopated with strong accents, so they remind you of Latin music. The ragas (or scales) remind you of blues or sometimes hip-hop. Singing is accompanied by drumming. And once you perform the basic rendition of your song, you go on and improvise with rhythms and pitches that are similar to scat singing in jazz or beat box (with your mouth). In Indian music you use the syllables *sa ri ga ma pa da ni sa* (which for us is "do re mi fa so la ti do"). I found the music to be mysterious and very wild, in that it is the singer's improvisational adventure. The singing style is truly dramatic, as a great improviser is no less theatrical than an actor doing a monologue, a great poet reciting at a salon, or a rapper going off on some wild tangent. The music never seemed remote to me, and it combined theater and music into one form.

I had to go through a number of stages in order to learn Carnatic singing. My teacher was named Kaliana Khrishna Bahvaktavar. First I had to learn to pronounce his name. Then, as his student, I was required to carry his instrument for him whenever we walked around campus. His instrument was a vina (a bigger version of the sitar with four main strings and three resonating strings). The vina isn't heavy, but it's made from bulbous gourds that made going through doors quite perilous. Besides carrying the instrument I had to play a droning instrument called a tambura behind Kaliana Khrishna Bahvaktavar (I never did learn to pronounce his name). I was to position myself way behind him during his concerts. The tambura has four strings that are tuned to drone and resonate nonstop through every song in the concert. The tambura is also made from a bulbous gourd, which I had to balance on my lap and stretch an arm around in order to pluck the strings to keep the drone going. No one tells you, but it's implied that if you let the drone stop, the world will come to an end and it's your fault. My final chore was to understand Kaliana Khrishna Bahvaktavar, though he spoke no more than ten words of English. Six of the ten words were "You are so beautiful, thank you."

During my first lesson, I sat cross-legged facing my teacher. He droned one long sustained pitch on the syllable *sa*. He continued to sing *sa* and invited me to join in. Breathing when I was desperate, I continued to hold that one singular long *sa* for the entire lesson. After two hours, Kaliana Khrishna Bahvaktavar nodded his head in that particular way East Indians do and said, "You are so beautiful, thank you." I left high as a kite from a lack of oxygen and returned the next week to do exactly the same exercise. My teacher sat with closed eyes and nodded his head up and down as if I were singing a full song. After two weeks, I graduated to two notes in succession. I never seemed to hear the two pitches exactly right. I *thought* I was singing the same notes that he was, but I was listening with my brain to what I *thought* he was singing. I should have been listening with my ears, skin, and eyes, and breathing with my full body. When you sing along with a CD of Alanis Morissette, Moby, or Faith Hill, you don't think to yourself, Well, now she's singing higher and now she's singing lower and now she's holding that note just a little longer and oops she just jumped off that phrase. Instead you incorporate the song into yourself and respond with your guts to the lyrics, melody, and rhythm. You move to the music, inside as well as outside, and every note becomes a story that is being told from one human being to another. When I studied Indian singing, I learned to give up my inner commentary and let myself be folded into the long notes. I could feel the vibrations from my teacher inside myself. And as we climbed up or down, from one note to another, I experienced my senses lifting or lowering with the sound. The process was so slow, I got to learn only three songs in the entire year I studied there. But I learned to listen to both my teacher's voice and my own in a new way. I don't believe I've ever thought about singing as "making the notes" again.

Many cultures teach chanting and singing without formal voice lessons or lectures on theory. Teachers can also make the written note full of personality. One teacher I had created a character for each note on the bass and treble clefs. In India the teacher speaks the beats to the student in syllables and the student repeats the syllables with the same rhythm and intonation. When taught well, speaking isn't separated from the function of the whole body. Once, at Bennington, I watched as my mentor—the great composer and teacher Henry Brant—taught his class a phrase from Stravinsky by having them hop up and down a staircase in the rhythm and intervals of the music.

If a student acknowledges the connection between body, spirit, and voice, he or she will feel less frozen when it comes to using his or her voice as a speaking or singing instrument. Yet there's so much we don't know about the voice. I'll never forget hearing a Tibetan monk singing two or three pitches at the same time—and not knowing how he did it. But most memorable of all was the time I saw a Native American actor actually break a wall with his voice. (It was sheetrock, but still . . .) Someday, maybe there'll be an event in the Olympics devoted to voice gymnastics. Voices will compete in jumping, turning, clicking, yodeling, dueling, and who knows what else.

There's nothing wrong with reading music—in fact, it's important to learn the code passed down from generation to generation in our own Western cultures. But no one should perceive himself or herself as inadequate if he or she can't follow notes on a page or doesn't know the standard musical notation symbols. Students have to learn to trust their ears. The division between singing and speaking is no longer rigid. Rap has taught us that speaking and music are one and the same and if you listen to a well-trained actor do a monologue, you can almost follow the beats and the melody.

An important method to be aware of is call-and-response. Call-and-response is used in music, political marches, cheerleading, religious rituals. It builds energy and allows a group to echo the enthusiasm of the leader. You shouldn't have to feel as if you must be very proper. You can play with the syllables as long as the vowels are clear and you make sounds that are simple enough for the group to repeat. Chances are if you make sounds that are simple and enthusiastic, your voice is being well used.

Note: All the following exercises are done in a spoken voice—not on melody.

General Voice Exercises

Aim: To hear the voice in its habitual tone, then to open up the vocabulary of the ears by hearing yourself expand your range.

Exercise 2.1: Students go around the circle and say their names. Then go around the circle and once again say your names, but this time make them strange and silly, exaggerating syllables, consonants, and vowels.

Example: My-eye n-n-nammme izzz Lllizzzzz Swa Swa Swa ddd ooossss. Ask the students in the group to listen to each sound. Has he or she ever heard it before? Can they hear the differences between one syllable and another? What's the difference between *ah* and *aw*, *heh* and *hee*, *oh* and *ooh*?

Aim: To create more sensitive imaginative listening without self-censorship.

Exercise 2.2: The director speaks a set of syllables to the group in a rhythm and then they imitate the sounds, beats, and *intention.* Intention means the impulse or energy behind a word, action, or movement. (This is an important word for the craft of acting.) Intentions can be very simple—loud, soft, slow, fast, high, low. But even these intentions are not as simple as they sound. There are some sounds that convey no recognizable human emotions. Think: what is the intention of a drum when it's playing a fabulous syncopated rhythm? The emotion doesn't have a name, but it does have an energy and thus an intention. Students shouldn't try too hard to think of human emotions before they make a sound. They should let the sounds develop out of them and see where they take them. They shouldn't prejudge the sounds or be afraid of what comes out.

Aim: To recognize intention through hearing rather than seeing.

Exercise 2.3: You speak syllables in different rhythms and tones with different intentions. The students imitate.

Example:

YOU: *Taka ti ta ka*

GROUP: *Taka ti ta ka*

YOU: *Taka taka ti to doo*

GROUP: *Taka taka ti to doo*

YOU: *Ka ti ka ti ta koh*

GROUP: *Ka ti ka ti ta koh.*

Ask the students to try to taste the sounds in their mouths.

Aim: To consider sound using other senses.

Exercise 2.4: Think of one of your favorite foods. Go around the circle and have each person say the name of that food with the deliciousness of its taste and texture in mind.

Examples: *Cheesecake, spaghetti, licorice, ice cream, French fries*

Aim: To translate the taste of sounds into syllables.

Exercise 2.5: Now think of that same food, but say a word that has no meaning. Put the same deliciousness into the vowels.

Example: Tachakoo *zaa* bee

Aim: To expand the sound vocabulary of consonants and vowels.

Exercise 2.6: Do the same exercise, only this time do it with foods you hate. Remember—don't use the face. Feel the taste in the mouth and put its bitter or sour flavor in the sounds.

Examples: Brussels sprouts, squid. Notice how different the syllables sound.

Aim: To expand the transformation of taste and intention onto syllables.

Exercise 2.7: Now take that same feeling of the sounds and put it in a made-up word.

Examples: Eyaganish, blonch. Syllables have tastes as well as sounds.

Exercise 2.8: Now go around the circle and have each person say a syllable to a beat, which the group then imitates.

Example:

LEADER: *Cha cha oh loh*

GROUP: *Cha cha oh loh*

LEADER: *Feekatomzi*

GROUP: *Feekatomzi*

Ask the students if the consonants and vowels feel different in their mouths. Do they sound cleaner, more decisive? As I've said, rhythms talk too. I've used the examples of a drum. As the body speaks, it becomes its own kind of drum.

Aim: To attach sound to rhythm.

Exercise 2.9: Go around the circle and speak a rhythm on a made-up set of syllables. Really acknowledge the feel of the rhythm. Is it straight and military? Is it off the beat and quick? Is it long and held out with a short accent at the end? Let the rhythm talk. Don't try to say an English sentence in translation. Let the rhythm have its own meaning. The group should then imitate you.

Example:

PERSON 1: *Akka day akka doo*

GROUP: *Akka day akka doo*

PERSON 2: *Doo doo doo cha*

GROUP: *Doo doo doo cha*

Aim: To keep a rhythm against others with sharp syllables.*

Exercise 2.10: Divide the group into four sections. The leader gives each section a different rhythm on different syllables. She builds up. Once all the sections are chanting at the same time, you should hear the different rhythms connecting and playing off each other. Ask the students to try to listen to the whole layering of voices while keeping their own part precise.

Example:

FIRST SECTION: *Aay yakka day* (this section continues all the way through, don't stop when the second section comes in)

SECOND SECTION: *Zo to me oh* (this section continues)

---

*This exercise is based on the Balinese monkey chorus or Ketchak. This chorus is done by fifty or so men who sit in a circle, with their arms linked, while one or two of them narrate a story. At a signal from a leader, the whole chorus comes in as rhythmic chattering monkeys amplifying the story. This storytelling is based on tradition, but now it is done as a tourist attraction. The rhythms and voices will inspire you: it's like fifty rappers going on at the same time. You can hear Ketchak on a CD called *Golden Rain.*

THIRD SECTION: *Ya ya ya meechola* (this section joins in and continues)

FOURTH SECTION: *Baaaaz ta ta ta* (the same)

Aim: To introduce the concept of dynamics.

Exercise 2.11: The leader conducts the four sections as the rhythms mesh. Then try loud, soft, fast, slow.

Now a student repeats the exercise and gives out a completely different set of patterns to each of the four sections. The group learns these syllables and rhythms. The students should be encouraged to keep each section clear and simple.

Aim: To expand the range of the voice.

Exercise 2.12: Go around the circle and have each person make a sound that is like a siren — up and down, sliding. Make the sound on each of the five vowels: *ah, ay, ee, oh, ooh.*

Aim: To expand the concept of pitch.

Exercise 2.13: The group does their sirens together:

1. On the same pitch
2. On a different pitch

Aim: To expand vocal technique with call-and-response.

Exercise 2.14: The leader introduces vowels but now with a short attack. Each time you exhale, you punch out a vowel (like military orders or a cheer). The group repeats.

Example:

LEADER: *ah   ay   ee   oh   ooh*

GROUP: *ah   ay   ee   oh   ooh*

Do this exchange several times and then add consonants.

Example:

LEADER: *ta   tay   tee   toh   too*

GROUP: *ta   tay   tee   toh   too*

Go through a variety of consonants:
> *ba   bay   bee   boh   boo*
> *ja   jay   ji   joh   joo*
> *ka   kay   ki   koh   koo*, etc.

Aim: To work on technique and listening.

Exercise 2.15: Continue with the same sounds. The director starts, then the group answers back. Now play with high–low, loud–soft, fast–slow. Go to extremes.

Aim: To give students experience in making up their own sounds.

Exercise 2.16: Go around the circle and have each member of the group lead a similar sequence of vowels and consonants. The choices and intentions of each student will increase the quantity of sounds available for their hearing and speaking. As their "vocabulary" grows, their voices will automatically become more flexible.

Aim: To explore a different technique while working on breathing.

Exercise 2.17: Hum together. Listen to all the *mmm*'s sounding at the same time. Try to make a continuous sound, so breathe at different times. Try to blend into one sound.

Example:

PERSON 1: *Mmmmmm* (breathe) *mmmmm* (breathe) mm

PERSON 2: *Mmmm* (breathe) *mmmmmmm* (breathe) *mmm*

PERSON 3: *Mmmmmmmmm* (breathe) *mmmmmmm* (breathe)

Aim: To expand breathing and make loud sounds.

Exercise 2.18: Calling. I'm sure you've heard one version or another of Tarzan's call: a long, sustained yodel that sounds through the forest and warns the elephants that hunters will soon be approaching. Unless your rehearsal space is equipped with vines, you'll have to practice calling under less exciting circumstances. But even so, the call can be strong, direct, and full of life. Students may think that making a long loud call requires screaming at the top of their lungs and shredding their poor throats into pieces, but this is a misguided notion. Tell them to shoot their call, like an arrow, directly toward a chosen spot. How they direct the sound is as important as its volume. They should try to open up and let the call come from the feet, legs, chest, and heart. Stay within the call; don't lose your connection or the call will die.

Have the students walk through the rehearsal space and call toward the ceiling, a wall, or a window. They should try to break the object of their call with their voice; it's been done. But do it with power, not shrieking high notes (that's a cliché).

Aim: To control the specific direction of the voice.

Exercise 2.19: The circle breaks up. Each person takes a partner, standing about three yards apart. One of them, the receiver, puts his or her hand up in exactly the position the Supremes used when they sang "Stop! In the Name of Love": hand vertical, chest high, palm outward. The receiver should imagine he or she is wearing the pad that a boxing coach wears to take punches from a student boxer. Now the second person makes a long, loud, sustained call right into the receiver's palm. (Don't yodel like Tarzan.) Students can use a consonant and vowel—*Yaaa zoooh veee*. The call should be directed right at the hand. The receiver should feel the vibrations of the voice on his or her hand. Now the partners reverse roles. They back up and call from a farther distance. Make sure they continue to aim for each other's hands. When sound doesn't have a place to go, it gets lost in open space—like smoke.

Now the same exercise is repeated without the use of the raised hand.

IN MY LIFE, I've practiced calling in spaces that range from the ancient ruins in Greece to the Metro in Paris; from a balcony on the twenty-fifth floor of the Tel Aviv Hilton to the Staten Island Ferry; from the stage of a Broadway theater to a bathroom in the Tisch building at NYU. Calling is my passion. Anytime I am involved in a show, I arrive early at the performance space and call my heart out. I aim my voice upward, straight out, down. I try to feel if the space has an echo or is dead. I try to sense how much room a space is going to give my voice to resonate. I get used to my voice being in that particular space and I test what I have to do to fill it.

Aim: To experience specific powerful sounds.

Exercise 2.20: Make short, long, loud sounds—a whole variety—into a wall.

Aim: To learn not to think about making sound.

Exercise 2.21: Stand in a circle. The director goes from one student to another saying *"ta"* up close so it's very one on one. The *ta* must be a strong syllable emphasizing the *t* and the *a* like the sound of a cymbal. The leader changes the tone and volume of the *ta* with each person. It's a game to see if the student can be surprised into spontaneity. After going around the circle in a regular way, the leader shouts *"TA!"* suddenly at whomever she chooses. The feeling is exactly like throwing a ball across a circle except a syllable is being thrown across the circle or to a student out of order. The element of sound frees up the voice. The exercise changes from game to sport to piece of theater.

I'LL TRY to say this mildly. Amplification is the archenemy of the theater. What if people were carried around by robots while playing football? To depend on a microphone is to insult the potential of the human instrument.

THREE

MOVEMENT

FOR MANY DECADES, movement in the theater has come to mean more than just dancing or mime. After all, an actor's body tells a story as much as his or her voice does. When singing, music is conveyed through the stance of the singer, the small or big movements of the hands and arms, and how the body responds to the notes and rhythms the singer is giving out to the audience. If you watch people in the street, you will notice that each individual's walk, pause, stop, start, bending down, or turning helps define that person's personality. As a performer, every movement you make—from the tiniest waggle of your finger to a leap through the air—has to be under your control as you remain aware of how this affects your whole body. The movement of the finger has to have equal energy and concentration as the leap, for elements of a story can depend on the smallest shift in weight. In Indian and Balinese dancing, the motives and emotions of characters are revealed by the direction in which they shift their eyes or the position of their hands. And the rest of the body is in sync with the part of the body that's moving. Again, I compare acting to sports—if your feet are in the wrong stance, it doesn't matter what your arms do when you throw a baseball or lift weights. The body functions as a whole, and ultimately the body and the voice are also one force.

A beautiful movement isn't always graceful or in slow motion. Nor is "beauty" always beautiful. A sappy ballet makes my teeth ache. If you watch men or women doing carpentry, or digging with a shovel, or lifting up a baby, or greeting each other, or even arguing, the body can be seen doing "beautiful," expressive gestures. A movement grabs our attention when it has purpose—and oftentimes that purpose is no more than getting from one place to another. A movement is an expression of energy. If you watch cats, you see that they move effortlessly about with great purpose. They never move for no reason; their bodies and their minds are one.

There was a Japanese actor in Peter Brook's international theater. His name was Katsuro Oida, or Yoshi, as he was called. I saw him bound up ladders, jump over the heads of a crowd of children, fold himself up into a big cardboard box, fall flat on his face, run around in a circle for what seemed like hours, and then sit so still he looked like his own replica in a wax museum. He could transform himself from an old woman into a nasty demon simply by how he stood. And when he entered a space, he could make himself virtually invisible or a shocking and vibrant presence. His body was his instrument, and for those present who were children or didn't speak English, his movement was a clear translation of the stories and emotions being presented.

Yoshi had been trained in traditional Japanese theater techniques. He taught us that at the core of this training was an exercise in which the actor simply walked in a straight line across a small rectangular carpet. As you walked, you were told to sense the beginning of the walk, the middle, and the end. The beginning itself was divided into "beginning, middle, and end," as were the middle and end. Yoshi taught us that this was called *Jo Ha Kiu. Jo*—the beginning, *Ha*—the middle, *Kiu*—the end. As Yoshi said, the purpose behind this way of walking was both complicated and straightforward. If you can sense

the beginning, middle, and end of a walk, then you can understand
the progression of a moment in time. You can be conscious throughout the whole movement and keep it moving forward, alive and energized. I once worked with a Korean director who talked about
"saving," which means that you don't put all your energy into the beginning of a movement and then trail off. Rather, you distribute the
energy in a way that allows you to stay focused and strong from beginning to end, saving enough energy so that it is distributed as needed,
as you move. I encourage you to read Yoshi's book, *The Invisible Actor*, which explains this in greater detail—as well as Peter Brook's *The
Empty Space*, in which he also talks about *Jo Ha Kiu*.

For me, this notion of awareness and build in a movement or
sound is related to music. Most good music "goes somewhere." You
can feel its movement from the first note. You hear phrases reaching or
building toward other phrases as instruments or harmonies are added
on. The volume grows or diminishes according to the direction of the
build; you can listen to a simple scale and feel the momentum. Although the literal direction of a piece of music or a movement isn't always faster, louder, or more complicated, the inner sense is "forward."

The arrangement of a song can be a helpful example of a build.
I think of moving to a song called "Try a Little Tenderness" as it was
written and recorded by Otis Redding in the 1960s. It's a rhythm-and-
blues gospel tune. It starts with almost nothing, but over a period of
six minutes it builds into a frenzied, impassioned vocal scream with
an orchestra of horns and drums behind the singer. You can feel the
tension in the beginning—you know from the first moment that you
are going forward and up. All along the way, instruments fold in, and
the rhythm and pitch of the vocal line become more and more intense. By the end, you realize that you've been moving, bit by bit,
toward the finish, never losing intensity or focus.

A good movement has a whole music to it. You simply want to
feel momentum, as if you're connected to the motion of your body or

voice as it moves in a natural direction. Ultimately, you want this forward motion to be effortless—the way a musical scale goes up or down. You will help your students memorize what it feels like to be in this state—not on automatic pilot, but always awake and moving. We are talking, once again, about awareness and concentration, but this time in motion. It may take them some time to reach the point where they get the notion of beginning, middle, and end, so they should first concentrate on making movements in which their whole body, concentration, and energy are involved, particularly since some students are shy about their bodies.

Specific Movement

Aim: To get rid of inhibitions.

Exercise 3.1: The whole group walks around the room. When the director says "run," everyone runs. When the director says "spin," everyone spins. Then they jump, lunge, and so on.

Exercise 3.2: The students walk around the room. When one student passes another, each says, "How do you do?" and reverses direction. Then each says, "How do you do?" and walks backward.

Aim: To get rid of inhibitions and begin to work on the physical imagination.

Exercise 3.3: The students walk around the room and the director calls out a situation that alters the walk.

Example:

1. It's too hot out, the sidewalk's burning.
2. There are bees chasing you.

3. It's hailing golf balls.

4. The sidewalk is pure ice.

5. That mud is sticky.

6. The bridge is falling.

7. *Shhh*, don't let anyone see you.

8. You've got to dodge those shooting bullets.

9. There're prickles all over this path.

(and so on)

Now that the students have moved without looking at one another, it's time to stand in a circle.

Note: In all exercises about sounds and movements I recommend that the students use single repeated movements. This helps concentration and focus.

Simple Choreography

Aim: To get in touch with familiar movements.

Exercise 3.4: Go around the circle and create some steps to a piece of music in your head. Teach the steps to the ensemble. Repeat several times.

Exercise 3.5: Match one or two syllables with a movement. Then have each student create a pattern with the sounds and the movement which he or she can teach the group. Repeat several times.

Example:
PERSON 1: Movement = step, turn, jump, wiggle
          Syllables = *ka chee la la ooh ooh*

Group repeats.

PERSON 2: Movement = bend knees, snap fingers, nod head
        Syllables = *zaka zaka ooh cha lay too*

Group repeats.

Unexpected creatures may begin to develop. Go with what comes naturally out of sound and movement. (Don't try too hard to make a movement you have seen and liked. I like students to discover what's unknown inside of them. It gets great results.)

Emphasize that "dance" can mean anything. You're not looking for jazz ballet, or musical theater. You want them to use steps they'd use in a club, or in their room listening to private music.

Note: In all exercises involving single repetitive movement, stress that this isn't just a physical "working out." Each sound and movement has to have an "intention" or feel. Repeat one single movement over and over.

General Movement Exercises

Aim: To isolate areas of the body and feel and concentrate on the energy coming out.

Exercise 3.6: Each student proposes a movement for a part of the body and the group repeats it. In the beginning, students should use only one of a pair of body parts.

Example:

1. Forefinger
2. Hand
3. Elbow

4. Shoulder

5. Neck

6. Head

7. Face

8. Chest

9. Waist

10. Hips

11. Thighs

12. Knees

13. Ankles

14. Toes

Aim: To improve coordination and develop inner focus.

Exercise 3.7: Now propose that each student make a move combining two unlikely parts of his or her body (again teaching the moves to the whole ensemble).

Example:

1. Ankle, finger

2. Knee, head

3. Elbow, nose
   (and so on)

Aim: To improve coordination, intention, and focus.

Exercise 3.8: Each student proposes a movement in which two or three connected parts of the body work together and then teaches it to the rest of the ensemble.

Example:

1. Shoulder, neck, head
2. Hip, knee, ankle
3. Chest, waist, hips

Note: Let the movements be repeated several times.

Aim: To recognize the separate parts of the body in the whole.

Exercise 3.9: Each student proposes a move with the full body, involving several body parts.

Example:

1. Squatting while lifting hands over head
2. Bending over waist, standing up, then onto toes, arms reaching upward
3. Head down, knees bent, arms covering head
4. Hands covering face, body stooped forward
5. Legs spread far apart, arms straight out horizontally, head in sharp profile to the side

Do the last three sets of the exercise to a beat. The beat speeds up and then slows down.

Aim: To be sensitive to the tempo of the body while staying aware of each individual part.

Exercise 3.10: Use one arm. Keep it to the side. Then, as slowly as possible, lift the arm up in front of you. Be concentrated on every cell as the arm is lifted. The group moves along with each student.

Exercise 3.11: Do the same with other body parts, moving to and from basic standing positions.

Exercise 3.12: Take a step forward, using the whole body, moving as slowly as it can. Then choose other movements to do slowly.

Aim: To concentrate on the energy of movement.

Exercise 3.13: Choose one part of the body and move it exceptionally fast. The ensemble follows. Then choose other body parts to move, the ensemble following.

Then make the fastest movement you can using the whole body.

Aim: To stay concentrated on a movement.

Exercise 3.14: Each student picks one movement, teaches it to the ensemble, and together they repeat it many times, concentrating more each time as the repetitions continue.

Aim: To acquire body and tempo awareness.

Exercise 3.15: Spread out the students in the room and walk as slowly and then as quickly as you can. Alternate back and forth between each extreme.

Aim: To feel the energy and shape of other bodies.

Exercise 3.16: Return to the circle. One student walks at a moderate speed toward another student across the circle. The first student should make clear toward whom he or she is walking. The second student takes the impulse from the first and starts to walk across the circle, clearly giving a signal to a third student. The key is to make seamless transitions without stops or starts. Therefore the transition between the student walking and the one who will take over has to be smooth and confident. Each student's walk has to be alive from beginning to end so there is no drop in energy level whatsoever.

Speed up this walking exercise gradually as the exchanges progress. By the end, the last student should be running.

Exercise 3.17: Do the same exercise with each student trying funny or distorted styles of walking.

Aim: To enhance group sensitivity and coordination.

Exercise 3.18: If you want, you can add a bamboo pole or basketball to the movement exercises, making sure that the energy of the student is transformed from the body into the object held.

Example:

1. One student lifts the pole or ball at a certain speed. The arms and object combined should feel like one limb.

2. Create a simple dance using the pole or ball.

3. Pass the pole or ball to each other with clear specific intention.

4. Fill the pole or ball with "electricity." As if it were a puppet, give the object a life of its own. (In this case, the body's energy goes *into* the object rather than the object being an extension of the body's intention.)

Aim: To combine the parts of the body and play with imagination and energy.

Exercise 3.19: Go around the circle again, and this time have each person make up a combination of simple moves to a steady beat. This is not about good or bad dancing; the key is to invent something so that others can follow it.

Example:

PERSON 1: *toe to heel, jump, jump*

GROUP: *toe to heel, jump, jump*

PERSON 1: *toe to heel, jump, jump*

GROUP: *toe to heel, jump, jump*

PERSON 2: *clap, spin, shake, clap*

GROUP: *clap, spin, shake, clap*

PERSON 2: *clap, spin, shake, clap*

GROUP: *clap, spin, shake, clap*

(and so on)

Aim: To work on movement and imagination.

Exercise 3.20: Divide the company into small groups. Each group should invent a sport and then teach it to the other groups.

Example:

1. Garbage-can race. Half the team has to crawl backward into a garbage can and the other half has to figure out how to get the garbage can to the finish line first.

2. Animal race (turtle). Different "turtles" from different teams try to make it across the room (the race may never end for some!). Or a fly arm wrestle. Elephant hockey—how do you push a puck with your trunk?

3. An acrobatic team that, instead of performing real gymnastics, ends up doing ridiculous, meaningless, stupid things, but takes a bow for each one anyway.

Aim: To learn how to believe in a specific physical world.

Exercise **3.21:** The student creates a very specific imaginary object. He passes it around the circle. The whole group tries to keep the object completely intact up to the last pass.

Aim: To learn how to believe in movement.

Exercise **3.22:** One person begins a very robotic movement. Another attaches his or her own robotic movement to the first action. One by one, each member of the company joins the "structure" until you have a whole machine going. The students should try to make the "parts" fit.

Aim: To improve spontaneity and physical interpretation.

Exercise **3.23:** One person goes to the center of the circle. One by one, members of the company call out aspects of a "monster" that the single actor has to embody.

Example:

PERSON 1: You have a humped back. (*The actor in the center bends forward.*)

PERSON 2: You have fangs. (*The actor adds fangs to his hump.*)

The students call out aspects and adventures of other creatures for the one in the middle to interpret:

1. Tree
   —attacked by termites
   —in a hurricane
2. Caterpillar
   —crawling on a log
   —turning into a butterfly
3. Vacuum cleaner
   —big mouth sucking in tons of dust
   —a coin blocks the suction

Aim: To achieve synchronicity in movement and interaction.

Exercise 3.24: Break up the group into pairs. The partners face one another and mirror one another's movements. No one should try to lead or follow.

The partners pick a repeated movement that they can do together. They do that movement very slowly, then quickly; sharply; smoothly.

One partner calls out a series of actions for the other to do. The requests speed up, then slow down. The partners try to stay in sync.

Example:

PARTNER 1: Sit down, stand up, turn around, jump backward, say hi to Suzi, touch the floor, fall asleep.

Aim: To improve imagination and timing.

Exercise 3.25: The partners split up. One goes to one side of the room, the other to the opposite. Each partner moves slowly toward the other. A physical theme develops and the partners move until they're very close to each other, playing out the theme.

Example:

1. Two cowboys menacing each other, waiting to see who will draw first
2. Two lovers happily reunited
3. Two relay runners, one passing the baton to the other
4. Two frogs going for the same fly
5. Two sumo wrestlers in combat

Aim: To enhance imagination and help create meaningful movement.

Exercise 3.26: The two partners create two-person scenarios in silent-movie style. The movement tells the story.

Example:

1. One starts to drown and the other saves him.
2. They fight over an object.
3. They try to dance together but can't.
4. One tries to walk more hip than the other.
5. They duel using stretched arms instead of foils.

Aim: To improve coordination between partners.

Exercise 3.27: The partners make up or do four steps of a ballroom dance.

Exercise 3.28: One student makes a photo, using two or three or all of the students. He or she manipulates the bodies. The image is frozen.

Example:

1. An old-fashioned family photograph
2. A war scene (from the newspaper or TV)
3. A moment in sports history
4. A bread and soup line
5. Miss America finalists
6. A political rally/protest
7. A religious gathering
8. A crime scene
9. A brawl
10. A dance hall

Exercise 3.29: The same exercise but the frozen image moves.

Exercise 3.30: The same exercise, but now the student adds a simple story and the figures in the scene play it out.

Example:

1. The family photograph

   —the baby cries

   —the brother pulls his ears

   —the mother leans over to talk to the brother

   —the father has to scratch an itch

2. A war scene

   —a soldier runs to hide

   —a wounded soldier writhes in pain

   —another soldier aims his rifle

   —another looks up in the sky for aircraft, then they all duck
   down, hearing a bomb . . .

Aim: To enhance imagination and a sense of the absurd.

Exercise 3.31: The students go off and put together a scene in which the movement is ridiculous. The "scene" is exaggerated to make fun of the people in it.

Example:

1. Acrobats bow and bow and bow, hopping on one foot as if it's a great feat, and bowing some more.
2. A team makes a touchdown and the guys jump, dance, wiggle, hug, and fall over one another.
3. A bad children's show, featuring big facial expressions and exaggerated movements, as if the children were stupid or insane.

SOUND AND MOVEMENT

Here are some exercises that combine the voice and the body. Again, use simple, repeatable movements.

Sound and Movement

Aim: To make movement and sound one intention.

Exercise 3.32: Going around the circle, each student in turn introduces a repeated movement for a part of the body. The student should invent a vocal sound that goes with or is inspired by the movement. Use abstract sound, keeping it simple so that the group can repeat it.

Exercise 3.33: Do the same exercise, but this time have the students use the name of the part of the body as the sound that goes with the repeated movement. The way the body part's name is spoken has to have the *feel* of the body part and movement.

Exercise 3.34: Combine the movements of parts of the body and their names, two and three at a time.

1. Elbow, knee, mouth
2. Toes, shoulders, belly

Exercise 3.35: Make a large flowing movement with a large flowing sound, then have the group imitate this.

Then make a sharp movement with a sharp sound, the group imitating.

Then make a loud movement with a loud sound, the group imitating.

Then make a soft movement with as soft a sound as you can make. Go on to tiny, fast, slow, high, low movements and sounds that fit them.

Aim: To enhance the coordination and dynamics of movement and sound.

Exercise 3.36: Combine opposite movements and sounds:

1. A large movement with a tiny sound
2. A speedy movement with a slow sound
3. A sharp movement with a long sound
   (and so on)

Aim: To enhance the combination of movement and voice with imagination.

Exercise 3.37: Each actor in the circle makes up a fake country and introduces a "folk song and dance" from that country. Again, make the choices simple so they can be taught.

Example: "I am from the country of Zigga Zigga and in Zigga Zigga we do everything in zigzags." I then begin a dance with repeated zigzag motions while making a song out of the sound *zig zig zag zag zigga zigga zagga zagga*.

Example: "I am from the country of Nnnooom and every third Friday of the month we sing and dance our praises to the holy Nnnooom fly who is our god of tickling." I then flap my arms in a speedy fly motion, hop on my feet, and make an extremely nasal sound (like a fly): "*Nnnnn mmmm*."

Sound and Movement in Groups

Aim: To create simple but diverse movements and sounds; to find the core of the movement and sound, while keeping loud sound in control.

Exercise 3.38: The students go off in different groups of three to seven and put together a band of their choice. It can be heavy metal, lounge music, blues—whatever. Each person chooses an "instrument" which he or she "plays," using the movement that expresses playing the instrument while creating the essence of the sound of that instrument.

This isn't about seeing who can imitate an instrument the best. The idea is to create a small world of overlapping sounds and movements that give off the energy of a band.

Example: Punk rock band

PERSON 1—Guitar

PERSON 2—Bass

PERSON 3—Another guitar

PERSON 4—Trap drums

Or: Jazz quintet

PERSON 1— Saxophone

PERSON 2— Trumpet

PERSON 3— Stand-up bass

PERSON 4— Piano

PERSON 5— Conga drums

Try to discourage the students from using music that already exists, but if they really get stuck, they can resort to their own arrangement of a well-known tune.

Exercise 3.39: The students do exactly the same exercise, but this time the students form a band in which the individuals sing. They make up one or two lines of lyrics, pick the style of music, and perform. In this case, the "mood" of the music should fit the lyrics.

This exercise is also about parody or satire. But it's best for everyone if the students genuinely try to capture the energy of their "band" and the essence of that style. Later on we will discuss how good satire is rooted in taking the object of your satire seriously and not just making fun.

Aim: To link sound to movement and movement to sound between partners.

Exercise 3.40: The first person makes a gesture and the second person a sound to go with it. Then the first person makes a sound and the second a gesture to go with it.

Example: One student makes a sharp punch in the air with his fist and the other goes *"oof!"* The other student starts with *"Bzzzt,"* and the first one waves her fingers fast, like moving flies or bees.

Aim: To identify the intention of abstract sounds and to free up the voice and body at the same time.

Exercise 3.41: One student makes a series of diverse sounds while seated, like a score for a cartoon. The other person moves to the sounds, trying to pick up what the intention is.

Example:

SOUND MAKER: eeeeeeech   uga uga   oh oh oh oh oh

MOVER: (*Up on toes, frantic. Belching. Lifting head up, turning head sharply, looking around*)

Or:

SOUND MAKER: hey   oooyaya   nanananana   Huh huh huh mmm

MOVER: (*Stops, body wobbles in slithery motion. Military march. Rubs belly*)

This is an improvisational duet: the students provide sound and movement instantaneously. Eventually, sound will feed movement and movement will feed sound, in an organic way. Just keep the sounds away from "real" words or speech patterns.

Exercise 3.42: Now add a second mover and sound maker. See what relationships ensue.

Example:

FIRST SOUND MAKER: eeeek huh huh huh   ayah ayah ayah oookooookooook

FIRST MOVER: (*Jumps runs   stands shaking fearfully*)

SECOND SOUND MAKER: aha   yaka yaka   oomph

SECOND MOVER: (*Comes up behind   laughs and chases crashes into other*)

Aim: To achieve synchronicity between one student and another, in movement and sound as well as in imagination.

Exercise 3.43: "Dubbing": One person speaks from a sitting position while the other does movement that captures the words. The sound and movement work together.

Example:

SPEAKER: Oh my darling, I long for you. Where are you?

MOVER: (*Reaches out arms. Gets on knees. Turns around, looks everywhere*)

Or:

SPEAKER: If I really pull—ugh—if I try—I can get this sword from this stone.

MOVER: (*Tugging motion, out of breath, bigger tugging, falls to ground holding imaginary sword*)

Exercise 3.44: The exercise grows into a scene between "two" people (actually four students). The speaker and the mover take turns leading.

Example:

FIRST SPEAKER: What is that in your hair?

FIRST MOVER: (*Looks in second mover's hair*)

SECOND SPEAKER: What? What?

SECOND MOVER: (*Touches hair fearfully*)

Or:

FIRST SPEAKER: Uh oh, it's a rat.

FIRST MOVER: (*Jumps back.*)

SECOND SPEAKER: *Screams*

SECOND MOVER: (*Tries to rip out hair*)

Or:

FIRST SPEAKER: *Laughs*

FIRST MOVER: (*Points. Shrugs*)

SECOND SPEAKER: Thanks a lot.

SECOND MOVER: (*Walks away, embarrassed*)

These exercises should go on only as long as the communication and flow can be sustained. If the "scene" starts making no sense, see if it might be altered to work, but stop it quickly if it doesn't.

Aim: To understand complex directions in sound and movement.

Exercise 3.45: Create a new sport. The players are divided into two or three groups. The "sport" can be nonsense, but it must be clear and have its own rules.

Example: In *Runaways*, we developed a sport that went something like this. There are two teams. The players are spread out in a large space, the teams intermingled. Players from Team A try to throw a basketball among teammates; players from Team B try to intercept the ball and pass it among their teammates. The goal is for one team, when in possession of the ball, to name more breakfast cereals (or types of car, or female singers, whatever the topic is) than the other.

Let's say the subject is "breakfast cereals." Sally, on Team A, throws the ball to teammate John. John catches it and starts to recite breakfast cereals ("Rice Krispies, Corn Flakes . . ."). Before he can pass the ball to a teammate, he is tagged by Max of Team B, who then gets the ball. Max recites cereal names until he passes the ball or gets tagged. The winning team is the one that names the most breakfast cereals.

FOUR

CHARACTERS

INVENTING CHARACTERS

THERE ARE many ways of "finding" a character or becoming a character. I don't believe that there is one definitive method. Stanislavski, Stella Adler, Michael Chekov, Jerzy Grotowski, Peter Brook, and hundreds of other teachers and directors have their different theories and styles. I think that ultimately it's best to work specifically—that is, create and find characters that are directly related to the theme and story of the show you are making. Otherwise, the work has no boundaries and becomes general and unfocused. If you are not making a show, the characters should be restricted to a place or theme.

What is a character? When I do youth-oriented theater, I ask my actors to create the physicality, the voice, and the mannerisms of the person or creature they intend to play. I do much work with the body, the rhythm of the person's timing, and how he or she would react in various situations. For instance, if I were asking an actor to play a stuck-up llama, I'd want him to find out how he thinks the llama stands and what it looks like when it's in a hurry. I ask, what does snobby sound like? Recently I did a show for Scholastic Publishers based on my book *The Animal Rescue Store*, in which a young person had to play such a llama. (In my imagination, the llama's face always depicts feelings of boredom and superiority.) The actor tried different stances using his back, and particularly his neck, as well as the heavy-lidded and quite bored facial expressions of the animal. In this work, "how much or how little" was the key. Did the llama speak slowly or softly or in a thick French accent? In a breathy voice, chopping off sounds, or dragging them out through the nose? With the tongue sticking out? Ultimately we came up with a snobbish llama that suited this actor's strengths and took advantage of his individual energy and imagination. I don't go into a rehearsal with young people having set notions in my head about how each one ought to act or what a character is like. The students and I find him or her—or it—together.

In most youth-oriented shows I have relied on my students' individual strengths, and I encourage them to find their own voices and movements, even making up staging for their characters. If the raw material strikes a true note, then I only help to refine it or make the work more specific. Sometimes I just leave the student alone.

For instance, when I created *Runaways*, I didn't begin the rehearsal period thinking to myself, "Well, Tom should play the graffiti artist," or "Diane should play the rich kid." I knew I wanted a graffiti artist and a spoiled rich kid in the show, but I chose to wait and see who developed more organically into that kind of character and who surprised me with improvs that brought to light whole new aspects of the character, of which I'd never thought. This left me open to incorporate the very original interpretations that any of the students might offer.

This approach also allowed the students to happen upon characters that were their own creation—ones that I'd never thought of—and therefore added a wider range to my show. I don't like work that encourages students to play adults, at least not the fully created classical or Broadway characters in previously written scripts. (I believe this kind of work is essential when one is studying theater history, but academic understanding and becoming a character are very different kinds of work.) What I'm saying is that when you choose to create a show—a show in which a young actor will be performing for an audience—this kind of "classical acting" comes off stilted or false. Any time I see a false mustache or period costume on a student, I worry. Does this role have anything at all to do with the experience of this student? Sometimes I'm surprised, but too often I've witnessed false and forced performance. Most of the time I think if an adult is being created for a scene, we know that for that moment, the student is being transformed into an adult. You might call this the "presentational" or more "Brechtian" style.* If outside playwrights are to be used, then it's best to employ one for a specific purpose—one who will sit from day to day at the workshops, watch improvs, and let him- or herself be influenced by what has been seen and heard in rehearsals.

I think this is one of the reasons students don't do theater on their own—the way they do play in rock bands and paint. Theater is often thought of as an "adult" form.

So, in keeping with the spirit I'm setting forth in this book, I will devote this chapter to explaining how students can make characters that they can own. And as you'll see, this doesn't mean that theater students end up playing only troubled teenagers.

First and foremost, the voice and movement workshops should be continued as you delve into this new work. The "instrument" of a student keeps growing, even as he or she goes deeper into the craft of making theater.

*The term *Brechtian* applies to the style of theater associated with the director Bertolt Brecht, whose work came to prominence in the 1920s in Germany. Books have been written about his work, but for the sake of expediency I will describe it as alienated, or belonging neither to the stage nor the audience—work that is seemingly objective but often ironic.

General Character-Building Exercises

Aim: To introduce the notion that you can be part of a person who is you but not you.

Exercise 4.1: Go around the circle and have each person tell a lie as if it's really true. The lies should get more and more outrageous.

1. My mother brands cows for a living.
2. On weekends I swim with dolphins and translate for them.
3. I have never, ever been angry.
4. I made my outfit today, including spinning the wool.
5. My grandmother was kidnapped by aliens, thus I am one-quarter alien.

    (and so on)

Aim: To introduce visual and aural memory.

Exercise 4.2: Standing or sitting in the circle, each student should think quietly about a person they've known or dealt with in day-to-day life. They should *see* the person, and then use all their senses to *feel* the person they see. After the image is clear, the student should speak and move in their own version of that person.

Example: If it's your sister and she chews gum and sticks a hip out when she stands—try doing all that. If it's a teacher who speaks in a very soft voice and walks around in high heels—try that. See what you remember. See what really captures the person, as opposed to faking a voice and movements you can't really do.

Aim: To understand emotion.

Exercise 4.3: Before too many exercises go by, the teacher should talk about emotions and the state of being. A person isn't always *just* angry or *just* happy. There are so many nuances and states of being in emotion; try to name some.

1. Happy but a little scared
2. Angry but almost laughing
3. Sad and angry
4. Curious and petrified

See how many "recipes" the students can put together. Ask them to write the combinations down for later reference. Peter Brook says that in his work he is searching for "emotional intelligence"—something simple and very real. Emotion is how our insides react and deal with our state of being and our memories.

Aim: To add emotional intention to movements.

Exercise 4.4: Dual emotions: Think about and then create a character who is feeling two emotions.

Example: I am a character who is laughing so hard I begin crying.

Exercise 4.5: Stand or sit in a circle and have each student, one by one, create a sense of character with his or her hands—*not* creatures or dancing fingers. Instead, move your hands in such a way that they seem to convey emotion or a state of being. Concentrate fully on the hands: no words or sounds. The second time, use sounds; for the third, use a few repeated words.

Example:

1. Fingers wiggle on palm

2. Fingers wiggle on palm with sound *ohoheeeeeeeeeenn*

3. Fingers wiggle on palm with words *ooohwhenshecoming?* when she coming?

Exercise 4.6: Do the same with the feet. The arms. The legs. The torso. The head.

The face should remain neutral. We want to discover how to represent emotion in a way that's not just "mugging" or making big faces that suggest stereotypical reactions.

Exercise 4.7: Eventually create an emotional state with the whole body rather than just facial expressions.

Example: Sharp movements with all the joints. Words: *I itch I itch I itch.*

Exercise 4.8: Now use the face as a mask. Create emotion by using the muscles in the face, not making faces.

Examples:

1. Jaw drops up and down, eyes blink with tics. Words: *I itch I itch I itch.*

2. Loose body shaking all over like a rag doll. Words (laughing): *oh my oh my.*

Aim: To use the body to create abstractions.

Exercise 4.9: Create a bizarre cartoon creature/machine/animal that consists of movements and sounds. This creature is strongly motivated, but who can say by what? Let silly sounds and movements be his own motivation. Two "creatures" at a time meet and relate inside the circle. Why is the creature energy so different from "human energy"?

Example:

1. Strange bird: A repeated movement of bending over and lifting arms, then hopping up and down.

2. Strange egg: Repeated movement of crouching and rolling, crouching and rolling.

Aim: To get to know a character in its body.

Exercise 4.10: Students should walk as their self-chosen human characters around the space. How would your character sit? Lean against the wall? Hide under a desk? Let your choice of character tell you how to move and relate to the whole space.

Example: My character is a very tired, somewhat sad slowpoke.

1. I sit slowly and then collapse into the chair.

2. I lean against the wall and then slide down because I'm too tired to keep standing.

3. I hide under a desk in a fetal position and fall asleep.

Aim: To imagine how a character would be in any situation.

Exercise 4.11: Pick a character and have him or her relate to:

1. Different weather: My slowpoke gets blown over and pushed down by rain and wind.

2. Different noise: My slowpoke turns his head slowly and yawns.

3. Different music: My slowpoke barely taps his toes and doesn't move any other cell in his body.

Aim: To become fluent in character motivations and voice.

Exercise 4.12: How does a character become who he is? What lies behind her choices or her moods? Go home and create a character for yourself. When you return to rehearsal, "introduce" your character to the group. Be prepared to answer any questions about your character, even if you have to make up the answer.

Example: Here's my character: Hewo I yam foh years old. My name is Lucy. (*Fingers in mouth*) I don't know what to say. OK well, I like Barbie's kitchen and me and my fwend Charlotte we make biiiiiig dinners there for all famous people and presidents, nurses, and cats. Sometimes I dwess in a fancy dwess Mommy bought it for me—yellow dwess. I spill on it. Mommy get mad. I cry. Oh well, dat's how it goes. Sometimes I get to wear dwess—like for Mommy's birfday—sometimes I like to lift it up and dance in a circle.

Aim: To get to know a character from a variety of dimensions.

Exercise 4.13: Each student should bring in a "relative" or "friend." Ask them to make a figure, someone very close to them, using objects, clothes, or artwork. The student should create the essence of their mother, father, sibling, extended family member, teacher, or friend.

Example: I'm bringing in my Aunt Teresa. She's incredibly two-faced. (I present a sock puppet with a nice face painted on one side and a nasty face painted on the other.)

YOU: Hello, Aunt Teresa.

AUNT TERESA (nice face): Oh, you are such sweet dears and it is so very nice to meet you. (*Turns the sock around*)

AUNT TERESA (mean face): Aren't they just *scum*. They smell and they look stupid too.

Exercise 4.14: After a focused examination of the created relative, have the student perform with their body and voice a live interpretation of the character he created.

Exercise 4.15: The student creates a similar replica of himself or herself.

Example: Joe is a skateboard nut, so he brings in a teddy bear on a piece of cardboard balanced on a toy truck (which is a kind of primitive skateboard). He talks about why this is important to him.

Example: Roger brings in a T-shirt pinned to a pair of pants, with the pants pinned to socks.

ROGER: This is my best friend Sam. He's so cool, nothing gets to him. (*Moves floppy clothes*) Is he loose or what?

Aim: To become more fluent with the character's being.

Exercise 4.16: Students come in dressed up as characters (I try to time this exercise with Halloween). They act the whole time without a break until I say they can stop.

Exercise 4.17: Students (as themselves) should ask questions of their characters, and then respond to their own questions as the people they've made up.

Example: For instance here's my four-year-old girl:

Q: What does your daddy do, Lucy?

LUCY: He makes trees grow, I think.

Q: Do you have brothers and sisters?

LUCY: (*Fingers in her mouth, gets distracted, wiggles*)

Q: Lucy?

LUCY: I haff to go pee.

Q: Should I take you?

LUCY: I haff two bros, Hawwy and David. I haff to pee bad.

Q: You want me to take you?

LUCY: Yes, but not now. I'm real hungry. (*Starts to fidget*) Where's
   my mommy?

Example: Yeah, my name is—I don't have to tell you my name. Who
are you? You got a cigarette? How 'bout some blow? Screw school,
man—that Mrs. Jordan—she's a bitch, man. So what? So I don't
come to class? Big deal. Me and my boys—we got bigger dreams. Oh
yeah. Right—like I'm gonna tell you.

Aim: To learn to change roles quickly and spontaneously.

Exercise 4.18: This exercise is called Box Transformation. Place a cardboard box on the floor, with both ends open so that your students can
crawl through. Students walk like themselves up to one end of the box,
crawl through, and emerge completely different people or creatures.

Example: Sally starts off as Sally as she goes through the box, but she
comes out the other end as an opera singer (or chimpanzee or robot).

   In the advanced version, "transformed" students crawl through
backward and become themselves again.

Aim: To work on spontaneity and imagination.

Exercise 4.19: A shoe or hat is placed in the center of the circle. Each student goes in and picks up the object and is immediately transformed into another person or creature. In other words, the shoe or hat has an instant magical power that transforms the student on contact.

Example:

1. Jim goes into the circle, picks up the shoe, and becomes a silly girl. When he puts the shoe down, he's himself again.
2. Sally goes into the circle, puts on the hat, and becomes a nervous, paranoid person always looking over her shoulder.

Exercise 4.20: In another version of the exercise, the shoe or hat becomes an object that the student uses in his or her choice of character. The object transforms the student but also becomes his or her prop.

Examples:

Rock singer: shoe, microphone

Weight lifter: hat, heavy weight

Unicorn: shoe, horn

A street person: hat, a hat for begging

The characters that come out of these transformation exercises don't always have to be easy to name or identify. A mood might change; a seeing person could go blind; a big shot might become a lost person. Similarly, crying could become laughing, nastiness could become kindness. Or the other way around.

Aim: To be able to visualize and create a character that's been written by someone else; to be able to adjust to any situation.

Exercise 4.21: The director tears a sheet of paper into small slips. On each slip she writes a brief description of a specific character. In the first exercise the student picks a slip out of the hat and, when her time comes, she becomes transformed into that character, but no one else knows what character she has. Do this first with only sounds and the second time around with words.

Example: Janet takes a slip of paper from the hat. When it's her turn to enter the circle (she has picked "braggart"), she puffs out her chest, sticks her nose in the air, and sniffs like a snob.

JANET: I'm the best, the total absolute best, no one is better than me.

The director's choice of characters can be closely related to the theme of the future show. Or the choices can be specific characters with a clear identity that are related to the story in some way. But in the beginning, the relationship between two characters should not be overtly set or defined, to let the students make what they can of the situation.

As three or four students enter the circle, exchanges become a possibility. Once there are five or six, the relationships become more relevant.

This is a list I'd use for a large group doing a show about bigotry and differences between people. Only one character is written on each slip of paper.

1. A nasty bigot who picks on people wearing sneakers
2. A person who laughs at curly hair
3. A scared victim who hides
4. An idiot who doesn't know what's going on
5. A person who tries to get people of the same size to come together

6. A person who is happy for mean people and mad at nice ones

7. A person who enjoys making trouble, and sets other people up to take the blame

8. A person who gets frustrated with people who laugh

9. A person who hates people wearing green

10. Someone who is scared of socks

11. A person who mocks people behind their backs

12. A person who hates everybody

13. A person who is proud of his or her sneakers

14. A person who is trying to find people who hide

15. A person who thinks he or she knows everything

16. A person who likes only people shorter than he or she is

17. A person who laughs at everything

18. A person who loves green

19. A person who loves socks

20. A paranoid who is always looking behind him or her

21. A person who laughs all the time

22. A person who loves everybody

You will notice that I steer away from conventional prejudice and use metaphors—sneakers, for instance, instead of skin color. This gives the students freedom to take their characters as far as possible without worrying about being offensive.

Exercise 4.22: Now try combinations of two characters. You will need a large circle for this exercise, which should be done with sounds and movement only. Otherwise, words will take over and the relationships will become shouting matches.

Example:

PERSON 1: A nasty bigot who picks on people wearing sneakers

PERSON 2: A person who hates people wearing green

Situation: Perhaps the nasty bigot is wearing some green or the person who hates green is wearing sneakers.

Action: They can try to avoid each other or confront each other. If no relationship exists, each student will look around the circle for the source of their scorn and derision.

Example:

PERSON 1: A scared victim who hides

PERSON 2: A person who loves socks

Situation: The sock lover is trying to look at the socks. The scared victim thinks the sock lover is trying to hunt him.

Action: The sock lover tries to touch the scared victim's socks and follows him wherever he tries to hide.

Example: Three students enter the circle.

PERSON 1: An idiot who doesn't know what's going on

PERSON 2: Someone who is scared of socks

PERSON 3: A person who is proud of his sneakers

Situation: Sneakers Person goes up to Idiot Person to show off his sneakers. Idiot Person has no idea what Sneakers Person wants and takes off his shoes to give them to Sneakers Person. Sneakers Person now goes up to Socks Person to try and show her his sneakers. Socks Person freaks out, thinking Sneakers Person is trying to get her to touch his socks. Idiot Person follows happily and offers his socks to

Socks Person. Socks Person freaks out again because she thinks Idiot Person is trying to show her his socks.

Note: If the students are keeping their characters' motivations clear, they should be able to respond as that character to whomever they encounter.

The teacher changes who goes in the circle, making different combinations and different numbers of students.

Exercise 4.23: The teacher tells all the students, in character, to walk around the room to see with whom they can join up. She gives the students enough time to get into relationships with three or four other people; sometimes related characters will find one another in the crowd.

Example:

PERSON 1: A person who gets frustrated with people who laugh, ends up with

PERSON 2: A person who laughs at people all the time.

Or:

PERSON 3: A person who is happy for mean people and mad at nice ones

PERSON 4: A person who knows everything

Action: Person 3 is very happy for Person 2 and smiles and laughs and runs into Person 1 (a person who gets frustrated with people who laugh) while Person 1 gets extremely frustrated with Person 2, which makes Person 3 even happier, and this causes Person 4 (a person who knows everything) to march over and lecture Person 1, Person 2, and Person 3 on how to fix the problem (even though she has no idea what the problem is!).

After many combinations have been tried, the teacher calls the group together, puts the slips in the hat, and has the students pick once more, beginning the whole process all over again.

Though this may seem confusing on paper, the exercise is really simple when students begin to take on the characters described on the slips.

Aim: To tie simple actions to a state of mind; to help develop another way to find a character.

Exercise 4.24: Put a mess of clothes in the middle of the floor. Ask a student to fold the laundry in whatever emotional or physical state his fellow students call out.

Example:

"You're furious." Student throws the clothes together, hurling each shirt into the pile.

"You've eaten too much." Student can hardly move and barely lifts a sock.

"It's your birthday." Student happily folds, quickly and efficiently.

"You've got poison ivy." Student stops constantly to scratch himself (or tries not to), and the clothes fall on the floor.

Aim: To bring to life an existing fictional character.

Exercise 4.25: Ask each student to think of a character in a story or book that they really love.

Example: The ugly duckling who becomes a beautiful swan.

Student waddles around, ashamed. Slowly each limb becomes a graceful limb, as she becomes beautiful.

Example: Holden Caulfield in *The Catcher in the Rye.*

Student walks with hesitation, rubs his eyes as if they burn. Shakes his head. Shrugs. Walks as if he's alone.

Aim: To physicalize a character, encourage spontaneity.

Exercise 4.26: Ask the students to walk around the space until a chosen student or the director calls out the name or description of a person and his or her job. Everyone finds that character and freezes in position.

Example:

1. Your name is Sam and you're a stingy storekeeper.

2. Your name is Hillary and you're a senator from New York.

3. Your name is Ralph and you work deep in the mines of Kentucky.

Aim: To observe the details of human behavior.

Exercise 4.27: Sit in a circle and have each person talk about a friend or relative, telling the group one aspect of how that friend or relative acts that has attracted the student's attention, such as:

wipes each dish twice

yells at the class

shows off at a party

punches or kicks

giggles when he talks

wears the same T-shirt five days in a row

sings in the kitchen

smokes like a gangster

The choice doesn't have to be dramatic or violent, but remember that abusive characters still have to be observed in the same detail as every other character.

After the student has presented this aspect of their person, ask the group to try to feel the way the person described was feeling. Talk about why you think the person described acted this way.

Exercise 4.28: The students do the same exercise, this time observing small things about themselves.

Example:

STUDENT: I bite my lip and tap my toe waiting for the bus.

Aim: To feel a character from the outside as well as the inside.

Exercise 4.29: Ask the students to dress as a character who fits a specific chosen theme. Have each dress up and come to class as that character. (Do not stop until the director says so; it can be a half hour or a whole class period.) Another day, choose a completely different theme.

Example: Poverty

1. Elna wears a skirt with a ripped hem and one old shirt over another. She lives in the projects with her drunken mom and has to take care of the family.

2. Tom has on a thin T-shirt and ripped jeans. His shoes have no laces. His character lives way out in the country, in a shack

made of tin and cardboard. He's stopped listening to anyone
and goes where he wants.

Aim: To relate to text in a physical way.

Exercise 4.30: Ask the students to read a play, and then have them
choose a character from that play and memorize one of the character's monologues. Then have them try to find a physical action that
depicts the character, followed by a repeated sound. Slowly add the
real words.

Example: Here is A.J.'s first monologue from *Runaways*:

> My parents lived together, but they hated each other. See, my father
> went to work, see he was the head of the family. And mom, it was her
> job to stay home all day and clean the house. And every night at
> about six o'clock, I'd hear the electric garage door open, and I'd
> think to myself: "Did I do everything right? Did I do everything
> right?" Then I'd hear him come up the stairs. This was it! Please
> don't yell, dad. Please don't yell. Then mom would call us, and we'd
> all go sit at the table. And there'd be silence. (*Pause*) Until my father
> would say something stupid. And my mother would break down and
> they'd start fighting, and she'd grab us and put our coats on and try
> to take us out the door, and my father would pull us back in and
> leave my mother out on the porch all by herself. And I was tired of
> being fought over. I had to go! I had to go!
>
> —*Runaways*, performed in 1977 in New York (New York: Bantam, 1979)

A.J. is a young, tough boy. His monologue is full of short sentences,
and immediate observations; the emotion is urgent. Without words,
a student might depict the physical action of the character by running in place, doing jabs and uppercuts, punching fast like a fighter.

Then the student could add sound, perhaps using short, sharp syllables with lots of consonants: *ta ta tatatatata*. Finally, the student
should recite the memorized monologue, doing the same physical
action and using the same staccato speech patterns. How does it give
life to the monologue?

Aim: To create a human/nonhuman character.

Exercise 4.31: One student sits and another sits on his knee. The one
on the knee speaks, pretending to be a dummy. The dummy tries to
trip up the "ventriloquist."

Example: Lisa is the ventriloquist and Sam is the dummy.

LISA: Hello, my name is Lisa.

SAM: Hello, my name is Lisa.

LISA: You're not Lisa, you're Sam.

SAM: No, I'm Lisa, Lisa, and you're Lisa too.

LISA: Sam, you're Sam.

SAM: Sam I am not, Lisa, Lisa, I am not Sam, I'm Lisa.

LISA: You're driving me crazy.

SAM: That's not hard to do.

Aim: To give character to objects.

Exercise 4.32: Use miniatures—little dolls or other objects—and
give them actions and speech.

Example: Jim has a miniature truck, a flat piece of gum, and a salt
shaker. Jim zooms the truck on the floor in front of him.

JIM (as truck): *Lalalalalalala*, driving along a country road, *lalala*.

STICK OF GUM: I guess I'll just cross the road here. (*Gum slides across floor, truck runs over it.*)

GUM: Oh no oh no *ahhhhhhh!*

TRUCK: Oh no, I drove over a piece of gum.

GUM: I'm done for.

SALT SHAKER: (*mourning over gum*) Oh my husband, flattened, and at such a young age. (*to truck*) YOU!

TRUCK: No, no, it was an accident.

These exercises begin to overlap with the skills in the next chapter: "Improvisation."

FIVE

IMPROVISATION

SONG: "EVERYBODY'S A BIGOT"

SHAWN:

Let's tell the truth
The Jews run the game

NICK:

Why are these blacks
Always screaming for rights?

ILAN:

Every time we get weak
And let the ethnics in

SHARON/DANICA:

We know what's pure
We know what's right

Repeat verses in a round. (Company stamps feet.)

SHAWN:

Let's tell the truth
The Jews run the game

They've got the money and power
They own the big names.

NICK:

Why are these blacks
Always screaming for rights?
They're drug addicts, leeches
They steal and they fight.

ILAN:

Every time we get weak
And let the ethnics in
We lower our standards
And we welcome sin.

SHARON/DANICA:

We know what's pure
We know what's right
Caucasian and Christian
Christian and white.

CHORUS:

Bigots everybody's a bigot
Can you dig it
You got to hate someone.

—Company improvisation, *The Hating Pot* (1982)

The ensemble, movement, voice, and character work already expose the student to a great deal of improvising. Improvising involves creating scenes and dramatic moments without a script. The drama comes from the imagination and the visceral connection within the actors in the ensemble.

Improvisation can be used as a way to explore specific themes or to challenge the students' intuition and instincts.

When I do improvisation with a student ensemble, I divide the actors into groups of four or five (or six to eight, if you have a large group) and ask them to work on a specific idea. I give them ten to fifteen minutes to sketch their "performance" out, and at various intervals I let them know how much time they have left before they have to stop. No one gets any extra time—even if they claim to be on the verge of a true miracle. I find student actors work better together under pressure from the clock.

I warn the students to work against their innate bossiness and pride, and as groups create improvisation together, the members get to know one another. Therefore, I'll often ask them to switch groups after each piece of work in order to rearrange the combinations of personalities.

I ask the students to work physically first and then with sounds. Whenever we use language, I try to keep it to a minimum: short phrases, repeated words. I want to avoid long general conversation because words can cover up real emotions. All of us, including adults, slip into clichés or sloppy language unless we practice or are endowed with a specific gift for monologues or rants. If I were building a comedy ensemble or a professional improv group, then I would approach this work differently.

Most teachers believe that an improvisation should have a story inside it, and I agree. But a fully fleshed-out conflict and resolution isn't needed for the exercises I'm suggesting. In this case, mastering the art of improvisation is not the priority. I try to create improvs that will take the students deeper into the theme and character, often as a prelude to writing. I tend to stop each improvisational presentation after two to three minutes so that the students learn to fill an intense, compact piece of time with what is needed and what is clear. It embarrasses any actor to ramble on and on, stuck in a meaningless conversation, though there are of course exceptions.

I ask the students to put down the content and form of each improvisation in a notebook. When we go forward to write a finished show, many of the improvisations will become the inspiration for scenes.

When I was working on a show about African American and Jewish relations called *The Hating Pot*, a wonderful moment occurred during an improvisation. Halfway through a difficult process, an Orthodox Jewish girl who'd never been in the same room with an African American ended up in a scene with an African American boy who'd heard only the worst stereotypes about Jews. (He hadn't met any.) They basically just looked at each other. After a long pause, they shook hands. Neither one had ever touched a person from the other's ethnic world. It was a stunning moment that came out of nowhere, and it became an essential scene in the final script. During *Runaways* we did an improv in which the homeless runaways were sleeping on a rooftop. Each was to "wake up" as the others slept and reveal a dream about his or her fears or memories. The dreams that the students actually remembered (or made up) were better than any monologue a playwright could concoct. I put them in the show—word for word.

General Improvisation Exercises

Aim: To give great passion and importance to something abstract.

Exercise 5.1: New sports. As in the chapter on movement, the students should divide into groups and each group should make an original sport that the members teach to the ensemble. Make sure the game is purposely absurd.

Example:

Name of sport: snailing

What you do: crawl very slowly

Competition: Who can crawl the slowest while still moving?

Example:

> Name of sport: sock switching
>
> What you do: break into two teams and be ready to switch your socks
>
> Competition: Which team can switch their socks the fastest?

Exercise 5.2: Bad circus. Each group goes off and creates a circus act that won't work.

Example:

1. Lion act with sleeping lion

2. Trapeze act with actors running into one another on the ground with imaginary trapezes

3. Ringmaster with the hiccups

Exercise 5.3: Gangs. Each group goes off and creates a gang, and then the gangs interact in an unusual way.

Example:

1. Different gangs "face off" to see which gang can make the ugliest faces and project the nastiest body language.

2. A gang tries to be evil but keeps cracking up.

3. A very terrified gang tries to protect its territory.

Exercise 5.4: A fashion show. Each group goes off and creates a runway show with the newest and best designs.

Example:

1. Messy-haired octopus (lots of arms active)

2. Fish in a tight evening gown

3. Sullen kid who won't go down the runway

4. A model who can't stand up straight

5. All the models compete with one another and then brawl on the runway

6. A model so in love with herself that she ignores the others and the audience

I push a group to come up with at least one movement or one pose, even if I make it for them. But I never let a group give up. This way they understand the style of improv for the next day.

Exercise 5.5: A gym class or aerobics class.

Example:

1. The leader goes too fast.

2. The class is rowdy behind the teacher's back.

3. The teacher has the students do strange things as if they were exercises (such as "Turn a doorknob, two-three-four" or "Flap your wings, two-three-four").

Exercise 5.6: A bizarre cooking class.

Example:

TEACHER: Now you take the moose's toe and roast it lightly with a sour milk sauce, adding brussels sprouts and pigeons' feet. (*The class falls deathly ill one by one.*)

Exercise 5.7: Take a text and, as a student recites it, have other students shout out the names of animals, requiring the reader to change into animals that have been called out. The reader will have to change several times.

Aim: To be imaginative and persuasive.

Exercise 5.8: One student picks a difficult state of mind. One by one the other students try to get her out of it, but it is up to the "impaired student" to decide which is the right way.

Example:

> Person 1 is curled up in a ball, shy and scared.
>
> Person 2 tickles the back of his neck.
>
> Person 3 pretends to have something beautiful to show him.
>
> Person 4 leans over on top of him, hums, and crushes him.
>
> Person 5 sings him a sweet lullaby.
>
> Person 1 chooses to be fooled by Person 3 and looks up to see what his beautiful gift is.

Aim: To experiment in tricking others (or pretending to be something you're not).

Exercise 5.9: Each student must make up an object or a pretense and try to get people to believe in it. What is the pretense? What is the pretender's routine?

Examples:

1. Jacob has a piece of dust. He shows how he can put it under Sally's nose and she sneezes. What a great piece of dust!

2. Max has a piece of paper. He reads it as if there's something incredible written on it. Everyone wants to see, but only the one who buys it can see what is written. Another student buys it and finds out it's blank.

3. Michael pretends to be dead. Mary mourns him, crying her eyes

out. Every time Mary cries, Michael "comes to life" and tickles her knee. She catches him and they have a huge fight. Mary gets kissed and now Michael is sorry. Mary tickles him as he cries.

4. Jane pretends to be a sweet bird. She coos and Rachel comes over to her to feed her. Jane the bird turns away; she is too shy. Rachel continues to tempt her with corn. Finally Jane the bird gives in. She sweetly moves forward to take the bread from Rachel—and savagely bites her.

5. Mark pretends to see a horrible bug on Sally's nose. Sally is terrified. She asks Mark to help her get it off. He comes closer and closer under the pretext of trying to get the bug off. He kisses her.

Maybe these examples will help the students come up with their own duping ideas.

Aim: To adjust to rapidly changing roles.

Exercise 5.10: Go off in pairs, and as in the character exercises in Chapter 4, create a "slave/master" scenario in which the master is cruel and abuses a slave. These images can be chosen from a variety of scenarios: from a depiction of ancient slavery; a lawyer with her secretary; an older brother tormenting a younger brother; a bossy teacher and student; an abusive parent and child. In the improv, the roles are suddenly turned and turned back again and again.

Example: The slave carries a rock. He trips and loses his grip, tossing the rock into his master's hands, so now *he's* the slave. The new slave hits the former slave with the rock and becomes master again.

Aim: To make a couple respond to each other and to external problems.

Exercise 5.11: Students walk into the room as couples. The director or another student calls out situations that change the feeling of their relationship.

Example:

1. One of you has cheated.
2. One of you has wrecked the car.
3. One of you wants to murder your partner.
4. One of you suddenly realizes the other is the most important person in the world.
5. You both get shot at; one of you falls dead.
6. One of you gets bored with the other.

Exercise 5.12: Different groups of students go off to create the structure of a family at dinner. They are to use the following props: plates, silverware, and glasses. They return with a version of their family meal.

Example:

1. Is it a happy family? All smiles?
2. Who is the favorite kid?
3. How do members of the family react to Dad being drunk?
4. Is someone keeping a secret?
5. Are Mom and Dad mad at each other and trying not to show it?
6. Does the family gathering blow up into a fight?

Aim: To heighten the group imagination.

Exercise 5.13: Divide the students into groups of five. Once again use the slips in the hat with instructions written on each one. Each person in a small group picks a slip that suggests one of the following situations:

1. You are attracted to someone.

2. You're trying to hold your temper.

3. You can't help teasing someone.

4. You're bored.

5. You have to go to the bathroom.

6. You have bad news that you're scared to tell.

7. You've got great news.

8. You want to leave the second you can.

9. You're ferociously hungry.

10. You have lost your wallet.

11. You're envious of someone's shoes, shirt, tie, or dress.

12. You're trying to be cool.

13. You're incredibly shy.

14. You think everyone around you is dumb.

(and so on)

The students reveal their characters or situations to one another. Each group creates a scenario that can encompass all five different instructions while they still inhabit the same place at the same time, and act together as a group.

Example:

1. You're trying to be cool.

2. You can't help teasing someone.

3. You're bored.

4. You have to go to the bathroom.

5. You're trying to hold your temper.

What unites the members of the group? They might choose:

1. A game of catch in the playground
2. Sitting in detention
3. Standing in line at the movies (or at a cafeteria)
4. Working on a cheerleading routine
5. On the subway
6. At a swimming pool

So they are all at the same place at the same time.

Example: In the game of catch, the one who is trying to hold her temper keeps throwing to others who won't catch the ball because:

they're too cool

they're bored

they have to go to the bathroom

and on top of it all, the one who is holding her temper is being teased by the one who can't help teasing her.

Exercise 5.14: Now subject each group of five characters to the same extreme weather condition:

1. Hot
2. Cold
3. Snow
4. Hurricane
5. Downpour

Example: Two students are sitting in detention and it's too hot in the room. The air is stuffy. They are sweating. Perhaps it's making them sleepy.

Aim: To achieve group spontaneity and cooperation.

Exercise 5.15: One group sets up chairs, tables, mops, and couches in an odd arrangement. The other group has to act out a "normal" situation using this set.

Example: A table is pushed against a wall and a chair is turned upside down, with a bucket in the middle of the space. A cardboard box is placed on the desk.

Solution: This is the scene of a bank robbery. Three employees walk into the bank to start the day, when two thieves with guns burst in. One teller is pushed against the wall with his hands up. Another is forced to go to the cardboard box (the safe) and transfer the money to the bucket, while the third is crouched down behind the chair, begging not to be shot.

Exercise 5.16: Give the members of a group unrelated props. How can they make a scene that incorporates all of the props?

Example:

an envelope

a shoe

a tennis ball

a piece of chalk

Solution: The students decide to throw a tennis ball and a shoe toward a line. They want to see which arrives first. Does the weight of the shoe slow it down? Get it there faster? One draws a line while the other collects the bets in an envelope. The shoe and ball throwers stand back, ready to begin the contest.

Or: One student throws the tennis ball and the person with the shoe tries to hit it with the sole (as with a handball racket). Another student keeps score by writing a number on the envelope with the chalk. The others watch and cheer.

Or: Hide the envelope in the shoe. One student desperately looks for it. Another acts like a psychic, trying to see where it is in a crystal ball (the tennis ball). The psychic helps the student find the envelope. The student pulls out the chalk, draws a dollar bill on the envelope, and pays the psychic.

Realistic? Abstract? Any use of the objects is acceptable as long as the students know what they're doing and why.

The Bread Improvisations

These exercises were used in Africa by Peter Brook. He found that the image of hunger and food was understood by all people. The exercises can be done with the whole group or smaller groups of students.

Aim: To work with a universal symbol to try to find universal scenarios.

Exercise 5.17: A group tries to share a small piece of bread equally.

Example: Here are some possible behaviors that could take place. These examples can be written on slips of paper or discussed beforehand by asking the question, What would happen with a group of starving people if they tried to get this bread?

1. One person tries to hoard it.

2. One person tries to run with it.

3. One person is shunned and not included in the sharing.

4. One person steals it and makes others do favors in order to get some of it.

5. One person tricks the others and distracts them, so he gets the whole piece.

6. One person passes out an equal morsel to everyone, leaving none for herself.

7. One person is put in charge of guarding what's left of the bread while the others sleep, even though she is so tempted to eat it.

8. One person surprises the group with the bread and there's general rejoicing.

9. The group decides to divide up into even camps, and the two sides create strategies to get and keep the bread.

10. They go to war.

Exercise 5.18: A piece of bread is thrown into the middle of the circle. Students react accordingly.

Example:

1. One person goes in and devours the bread and then is sad it's gone so fast.

2. One person walks slowly, fearfully, toward it, then finally gets it, and eats it in great fear.

3. Two people see the bread in the center, so they face off like two cowboys and mutually dive for it.

4. One person tries to decide whether to share it with a starving friend.

5. One person shares it easily, but the friend steals the bread from him.

6. One person greedily holds on to the bread, giving away crumbs to two others. Finally they go for him.

7. Two people share a piece of bread, then a third comes along. The two are divided in opinion: share or not share?

8. Two people share a piece of bread, a third person comes along, and the first two make him entertain them or do chores for them. Only then do they give him a little piece.

9. One person is savoring a piece when two people come along, one carrying the other, who's half starved to death. The first person gives the whole piece to the sick man.

10. One person gives up his bread to stop a baby from crying.

11. One person takes the bread from a baby.

12. Two people fight over the bread, but they're so exhausted that they can barely lift their arms. After a while they collapse, and a third person comes and takes the bread.

The director can think up his or her own situations in which to use a piece or loaf of bread. The same set of exercises may be done with water. These exercises also give students a tiny window into a reality they may or may not have thought about.

AFTER AN HOUR of improvs that require adversarial positions or a contentious atmosphere, the leader should stop early and get the group to start a tennis ball game or play music to which the students can dance. I try to prevent students from leaving my workshops upset by the contents of an improv.

IMPROVISATION WITH WORDS

If the leader gives the students a strong foundation in body work, voice, characters, and improvisation, then the student will be ready to do some simple improvisation with words. Before this work, a student would have been more likely to pick lines and situations that come from sitcoms or music videos. They'd use the words they heard in the media, and so would be basically just imitating others. They are also imitating phony "deep" emotions. Most artists do this until they find their own voices. But first things first. Students should have an understanding of the value of simplicity before venturing to do verbal improvisation. When they improvise dialogue, it's important that they listen to the other students' words and tone as well as watch their body language. The exercises that follow are intended to exaggerate reality so that the students can relax into them—enjoy doing them while remaining alert to others.

Solo Improvisation Exercises (Verbal Only)

Aim: To create a simple drama quickly.

Exercise 5.19: The student should gather several small objects (a pen, a salt shaker, a matchbook, a key ring, a glass; any small object will do) and then sit on the floor, placing the objects in front of her. Now she gives each object a voice and creates a scenario, moving the objects around in a miniature drama.

Example:

GLASS: Well hello, matchbook.

MATCHBOOK: Hello, glass.

GLASS: I hope you haven't been out lighting up cigarettes again.

MATCHBOOK: You should talk—you stink of beer.

GLASS: That's better than giving off smoke.

SALT SHAKER: Has anyone seen my French fries?

PEN: Hey, you're a glass and a matchbook, I'm going to write you a ticket for smoking and drinking.

GLASS: (*to matchbook*) I knew you were trouble.

MATCHBOOK: I haven't even burned it!

SALT SHAKER: Has anyone seen my French fries?

Aim: To maintain focus while changing the behavior of a character.

Exercise 5.20: The student recites a poem or monologue or talks about her day. As she is doing so, the following situations can take place. The content of her talk doesn't change.

1. She gets a bad itch.

2. She slowly turns into a chicken.

3. She goes in and out of a made-up foreign language.

4. She changes her mood rapidly.

5. She grows older / becomes younger / gets sick / tries not to laugh.

6. She tries not to cry, while still never stopping talking.

Exercise 5.21: This is an exercise similar to those in earlier chapters, such as Exercise 1.13, only more advanced. The details of each choice should be evident by now. The student talks about her day or what she ate—any casual talking will do. Other students call out characters to her, and she must take on these characters. The change from character to character should be instantaneous, allowing no time to think. The content doesn't change.

Example:

1. Toddler

2. Drunk

3. Beauty queen

4. Dictator

5. Politician

6. Army sergeant

7. Aerobics instructor

The students themselves will come up with many ideas. Try not to bring in suggestions that are vague or impossible to act out, such as mother or father (too general), or a shoe salesman who's actually selling beans that will turn into a beanstalk (how can someone convey that while talking about her day? It's too much information).

Aim: To acquaint students with complex human reactions.

Exercise 5.22: A double meaning—or subtext—exercise (an advanced version of the earlier exercise). A student speaks to the group about an event, opinion, or other person in one tone, but his underlying feelings are quite different. The leader uses this exercise to introduce the notion of complex emotions, contradictory emotions, and hidden motives.

Example:

STUDENT: I had a really nice time at Jane's party. There were a bunch of really rad guys and the music was terrific and I met a whole group of the coolest new friends.

Hidden emotion: Fear that no one liked him and he was completely left out.

Example:

STUDENT: Man, you look great. Those jeans look fabulous.

Hidden emotion: Why can't I have jeans like that? I deserve them more than she does.

Example:

STUDENT: I don't care about that test. I don't care if I passed or
    flunked. It's no big deal to me.

Hidden emotion: I couldn't understand half the words.

Exercise 5.23: Now do the same exercise as a game. A student picks
a slip of paper from a hat on which is written his assigned subject and
emotion.

Example:

    Proud: brags about father
He picks the hidden emotion from another hat:

    Lonely

The student puts the two states of being into a presentation that expresses the assigned subject while simultaneously conveying the un-
dertone of the assigned emotion.

Exercise 5.24: Another more recognized version of this game is to
put a subject in one hat and a situation in another:

    subject: favorite food

    situation: on a bucking bronco

Aim: To learn to keep attention and articulate what you are feeling;
to learn how to respond quickly.

Exercise 5.25: The student lectures on something he knows nothing
about.

Example:

STUDENT: I have studied the hummingbird for years. And I have
found that it hums when it approaches a flower to let the flower
know it will be taking its pollen. This is called the Hummingbird
Courtship Hum, and hummingbirds hum like this in Finland,
where the pollen has just a taste of white chocolate in it.

This improv becomes a "press conference" when the students ask
questions the lecturer *must answer.*

Example:

Q: Do the hummingbirds get eaten by other, bigger birds?

A: Usually not, because they would hum in the stomach of the birds
and make it quite uncomfortable. Squirrels can be dangerous to
hummingbirds because they have nutshells in their pockets,
which protect their stomach lining from the hummingbird.

Q: Do hummingbirds feel love?

A: Absolutely yes.

The speech and press conference can be on any subject.

Aim: To develop quick thinking and the ability to be absurd.

Exercise 5.26: Accepting an award. The student can do a general lead-
up to an awards show while using his imagination to come up with the
details (the student can choose his own award or pick it from a hat).

Example:

STUDENT: Thank you for giving me this Golden Vacuum Cleaner
award. I knew when I was vacuuming those rugs in the White

House that my country would be a cleaner place and this made me proud. And I'd like to thank my daddy for giving me my first vacuum cleaner. It wasn't gold but it sure was precious.

Exercise 5.27: Have the students improvise other fanciful or absurd first-person monologues, such as:

1. A political speech
2. A confession of a crime
3. A eulogy
4. A dedication of a new building or ship
5. An analysis of a sports event by the winning or losing player

Partner Improvisation Exercises (Verbal Only)

Aim: To learn to combine physical reality with verbal facility.

Exercise 5.28: Two students must "survive" a chosen situation, which has been either given to them or chosen from a hat.

1. A sleet storm
2. Being discovered by the CIA

Exercise 5.29: Two students debate something trivial.

PERSON 1: I think toothpicks should stay this natural wooden color.

PERSON 2: You forget that brighter colors make a happier day.

Aim: To truly communicate without generalizing.

Exercise 5.30: One student tries to convince another that the other is:

1. Being stupid
2. Hurting himself

3. Hurting another's feelings

4. Getting into bad trouble

5. Good enough to talk to another girl or boy

6. Brave enough to get through an obstacle or trauma

Aim: To work on a subject close to home; to deal with familiar subjects with imagination.

Exercise 5.31: Two students talk over a familiar situation. Using more stylized exercises, the situation can be assigned or taken from a hat.

1. Two students both want the same boyfriend or girlfriend. They have to talk it out.

2. One student is "cool" and the other wants to be his or her friend.

3. One student is passionate about going to the movies while the other wants to watch a music video. They have to compromise.

4. One student was sure he heard the other say something bad about him. The other denies it. They have to work it out.

5. One student thinks he won; the other student believes he won. They have to work or fight it out.

Exercise 5.32: Now one student tries to convince another in an even more urgent situation:

1. One student tries to convince another to have sex.

2. One student tries to convince another to steal or join a gang.

Partner Improvisation Exercises (with Movement)

From now on, words are no longer the only element that can be used. The students should go back to using movement and silence as well as talk.

Aim: To take the preceding exercises in this chapter and apply them to daily life. *Using movement.*

Exercise 5.33: Competition between two or three students. Debate with talk and movement over who's:

1. Stronger
2. More beautiful
3. Smarter
4. More miserable
5. More tired
6. More popular
7. More crazy
8. More angry
9. More in love
10. Meaner

Aim: To use technique (memory) and emotional intensity simultaneously.

Exercise 5.34: Name calling (an improv and memory exercise). Call each other's name. Then call more names.

Example:
PERSON 1: You are stupid.
PERSON 2: You are stupid and mean.
PERSON 1: You are stupid, mean, and lackadaisical.
PERSON 2: You are stupid, mean, lackadaisical, and smelly.
PERSON 1: You are stupid, mean, lackadaisical, smelly, and rotten.
PERSON 2: You are stupid, mean, lackadaisical, smelly, rotten, and a coward.

They should go on as long as they can.

Now use compliments.

Example:

PERSON 1: You have nice eyes.

PERSON 2: You have nice eyes and curly hair.

PERSON 1: You have nice eyes, curly hair, and a mysterious smile.

PERSON 2: You have nice eyes, curly hair, a mysterious smile, and you make me sing.

Or mix the two together.

Aim: To include two intentions when speaking.

Exercise 5.35: First meeting. Two students pick up slips of paper with occupations written on them. The students "meet for the first time." Each has to figure out what the other does, giving hints but never directly asking or telling.

Example:

PERSON 1 (optician): Hi, my name is Ted.

PERSON 2 (baseball player): Mine's Louise.

PERSON 1: Nice day. Can you see what a nice day it is?

PERSON 2: I know I'll be working on a day like this.

PERSON 1: The light really shines into your eyes on a day like this.

PERSON 2: First, of course, I gotta change clothes. Y'know, into pads and stuff.

PERSON 1: How can you see which clothes are what?

PERSON 2: Well, it's pretty obvious, man. I got a hat, see. I have to wear it.

PERSON 1: Do you wear anything to protect your eyes?

PERSON 2: And I gotta carry things—a wood-type thing.

PERSON 1: You'd probably see better if you protected your eyes.

PERSON 2: You should see the cleats on my shoes.

PERSON 1: You should protect your eyes. Get them examined.

PERSON 2: I gotta run over a big field. Sometimes I wear a big fat thing on my hand. That sure can cover the sun and catch things once in a while too.

Aim: To work on inner transformation and recognize human nature through exploration of other creatures.

Exercise 5.36: Assign each student a kind of animal, then name a situation that involves a group of people: a party; choir practice; a sport; a family meal; being on the subway; in a restaurant; on the beach. As the students improvise the activity, they move and talk like humans but their innate nature is animal. They carry the exact characteristics that would define the animal.

Example: Situation: a party.

SPARROW: Guest is nervous and responds to each sound and movement.

BEAR: A guy with a loud voice barrels through the crowd telling stupid jokes.

SQUIRREL: A guest sits very straight, very still—and looks around intently every so often but speaks softly.

SLOTH: Someone asleep, leaning on the door.

OWL: The guest is quite paranoid, often turning his head to see who's talking.

SNAKE: A guy coming on to all the girls, charming but with smooth, slippery words and gestures.

LLAMA: Someone just too full of herself to care.

ISSUE-ORIENTED IMPROVISATION

I rarely encourage students to "confess" if we are doing improvisations about real life. As I've said, I don't believe that a leader has to provoke pain or nervousness in a student to achieve a moment of high emotion. When touching on the most sensitive topics, I ask the students to act with sound and movement before using words. Also, I discourage the students from using clichés or imitating teachers' and parents' words. Despite the way teenagers behave, most are still deeply connected to adults. If we go into areas of trouble, we should do so as an ensemble. Don't lighten or simplify issues, but don't feel the students have to confess either. They simply have to make their stories believable—even if just to themselves, because the core of the theme is often true.

I try to stay very attuned to the feeling in the room. Remember that situations and feelings can be interpreted from either serious or humorous points of view but that humor sometimes cuts deeper. During the exercises, the students should be reminded that, in addition to humor, they have a whole stylized vocabulary of movement and sound now at their disposal. So if they don't feel that conversation is right, they can and should use other techniques, such as making sounds without words, putting their bodies into a position that becomes a picture of their situation, or using rhythm in sound and movement to convey the emotional content.

Issue-Oriented Improvisation Exercises

Aim: To bring truth to complicated issues.

Exercise 5.37: One student comes to another student, who is playing an adult. The first student has a terrible secret and she needs someone to help her. The conversation can go in various ways, which should be improvised:

1. The adult gets the secret out and wants to help.
2. The girl confesses the secret and the adult is punitive.
3. The girl almost confesses the secret but can't really tell it straight out.
4. The girl is intimidated into silence.

Aim: To find a way to talk to someone who died violently or is in the midst of a physical crisis.

Exercise 5.38: One student lies silently on the floor while other students approach and talk to the body.

Example:

1. "I told you that crank was bad."
2. "Why'd you run off with that gang anyway?"
3. "Why didn't you tell me? I would have helped you."
4. "Okay. So you didn't want to stick around. Thanks a lot."
5. "Mom made me come here, but I don't know why. You were never there for me."

Aim: To find ways to comfort and instill confidence in an introverted person.

Exercise 5.39: A student sits huddled in a tight ball. Different students do what they can to get her out of it.

Example:

1. "I'm sorry I hit you."
2. "I didn't mean to touch you that way."
3. "Hey, chill. I was just kidding around."
4. "Don't you play the child with me. You're faking."
5. "You get up now or I'm gonna kick you."
6. "Come on, I'll bring you a super-duper double cheese-bacon-guacamole burger with triple fries."
7. "Come on, let's at least talk about it."

Exercise 5.40: Two students sit staring at a bong or reefer or pipe.

Example:

1. They talk each other out of using it.
2. One talks the other one into it.
3. One talks the other one out of it.
4. They go for it in a big way and look stupid or scary when they get stoned.
5. They do it and explain what pressures and terrors they're trying to hide from.
6. They like it but they're stupid and say stupid things.

Exercise 5.41: A group of students improvise a binge drinking scene.

Example:

1. They pour (imaginary) liquor or beer down each other's throats.

2. A group tries to tease one student into drinking.

3. A group gets into a car—smashed.

4. The group tries to convince a girl to dance, or take off her clothes.

5. A guy comes on to a girl who's drunk.

6. Vice versa.

7. Fights resulting from the above.

8. A girl or boy wakes up with not a clue as to what happened. But it was bad.

Exercise 5.42: A male or female gang challenges a new recruit to do a number of actions to be admitted into the gang (steal, beat, slash, etc.).

Example:

1. The student refuses.

2. The student is reluctant but is swayed by "brotherhood" or "sisterhood."

3. The student is reluctant but is intimidated into doing what is asked.

4. The student refuses and dares to tell them they're jerks.

5. The student talks his way out of it.

6. The student enthusiastically accepts and gets into the details of what they want.

7. The student accepts, too scared to disobey.

8. The student wants to do even more than the gang asks.

Exercise 5.43: Hot male or female students tease a nerd. Depending on the nerd's reactions, the others either let up or act even worse. The nerd:

1. Is ashamed

2. Is defiant

3. Becomes violent

4. Goes crazy

5. Stays cool

6. Laughs

7. Makes a joke

8. Does something stupid

Exercise 5.44: An intervention. Family and friends surprise a student (who is acting like an addict) and tell the student (in improvisation) how his or her actions have hurt them. The student's reaction varies:

1. He resists completely.

2. He is defensive but admits to a "little problem."

3. He's defensive and blames everyone else.

4. He admits to his addiction just to get them out of his hair.

5. He gives in.

Exercise 5.45: Improvisation addressing pregnancy.

1. A girlfriend tells her boyfriend she is pregnant.

2. A girl tells her mother she is pregnant.

3. A girl tells her parents she is pregnant.

4. An underage girl tries to get an abortion.

5. A girl, much to her parents' dismay, decides to have the baby.

Exercise 5.46: Improvisation addressing homosexuality.

1. A gay student is hazed and mocked.

2. A gay student walks the halls with pride.

3. A gay student walks the halls with too much attitude.

4. A gay girl comes out to the boy who's been her boyfriend.

5. A gay boy comes out to the girl he's been dating.

6. A gay student comes out to his or her parents.

7. A gay student tries to cover up being gay.

Exercise 5.47: Improvisation involving a student who finds out he is HIV positive. His reaction varies:

1. He tells his friends.

2. He tells his parents.

3. He tells no one.

4. He denies it to himself.

5. He needs someone to tell, but has no one.

6. He tries to confide — but can't.

Exercise 5.48: If the social climate is right, ask a white student, an African American student, and an Asian student to trade mannerisms and ethnic clichés.

Exercise 5.49: Improvisation addressing marriage.

1. Two students break it to a third that they are getting a divorce.

2. Students re-create a custody battle.

Exercise 5.50: Improvisation focusing on the Internet.

1. Conducting flirtations on the Internet

2. Going to meet a stranger you've met on the Internet

3. Having communication that is getting more and more weird

4. Buying guns

5. Finding neo-Nazi groups

6. Finding eating disorder groups

Exercise 5.51: Improvisation focusing on fosterhood. The group divides into sections, which stand apart. Each section takes on its own identity as a foster home. A student who is "the child" gets passed from section to section.

Exercise 5.52: Improvisation focusing on crime. Each student writes or improvises a monologue about the crime that put him in jail, why it happened, and what his attitude is about it.

THE CHOICE OF exercises will vary greatly from district to district, neighborhood to neighborhood, even city to city. The negative elements that teenagers have to deal with are almost boundless, so exercises focusing on them have to be tempered with sweeteners and humor. As it is, I think the next chapter may be too real for many students. I've worked with students who have done improvisations centered around child prostitution and pimps, chicken hawks and old men, homelessness, being burnt out, being freaked out, being in prison or another institution, and other street realities. Of course, racial differences go on my list of improv subjects as well, but they can be focused specifically on the ethnic groups at hand. Still, there's often a remarkable energy coming from such a mix—as for instance in New York, where there's also a huge problem with all races and religions. I've also led improvs on other painful subjects: flunking math, disappointing an ambitious father, having a neurotic mother or an abusive older brother, dressing wrong, fighting to the death to get into high schools and colleges. Emptiness. Loneliness.

The one problem all drama students have is trying to depict how they live from day to day in this confusing, overwhelming, and always surprising world. They don't always know what's troubling them; they can't hit on what's scaring them. Therefore, it's important to recall and describe the incidents and atmosphere that have had a dark effect on them in an objective and factual way. Once they understand their own generation more clearly and view the world around them in a more complex way, they can use their empathy to create characters with new depth. This leads me to the next chapter, on discussion. I leave it until the last hour of the day, when acting doesn't seem to be enough. It's then that we sit in a circle and talk.

SIX

DISCUSSION

GINA: . . . So for the beginning we wrote down our topic on a single piece of paper and one of you can choose from the hat and then we'll talk about the topic we'll choose. If you really despise the topic you've chosen, you can put it back in the hat and choose another. Now, who chooses first?

AMANDA: I will. School.

JENNA: No. No, boring. Put it back.

MICKEY: Body image. No, no, not that. We did that already.

SARAH: Spirituality.

EVERYONE: (*Groan*)

GINA: Now stop this. You have to pick something. Make up your own topic, for godsakes.

EVERYONE: Shopping!

(*The girls have a great time making fun of fashion models.*)

GINA: That's deep.

JOYCE: Barneys.

RACHEL: Macy's.

SARAH: Estée Lauder Forever perfume.

CHLOE: Calvin Klein.

ANNIE: H&M.

AMANDA: BCBG.

MICKEY: Juicy.

REBECCA: Steve Madden.

AMANDA: Leah's Salon.

NESSA: Betsey Johnson.

MICKEY: OK, so let's say I have $50 to spend.

REBECCA: $50? You can't get a sandwich for under $50!

AMANDA: My mom won't let me buy anything under $200 because she thinks it's cheap.

(They break into their regular selves and begin to hang out.)

MICKEY: I can't shop with other people. I have to be alone.

JOYCE: I've never been able to make a conscious choice not to care.

CHLOE: I want to get the old snake eye, the look other girls give you if you're looking good.

REBECCA: You got to be honest. You've got to be truthful if they look bad.

ANNIE: I used to wear boys' clothes but I got teased a lot, so now I care more about what I buy.

CHLOE: I am so insecure. It's so intense, loud music, colors, intense sales people. My body heats up, I can't breathe. I'm trying to pick the perfect outfit.

MICKEY: I totally dress to please other people.

RACHEL: My mom insists on buying me stuff. She makes me wear it, I change it all at school . . . Don't show skin!

CHLOE: Here's what I love—boobs! It was a very big deal when I got my boobs. I'd been waiting for them. I got much happier when they started growing. I'd be nothing without my boobs.

—girls' own improv from *Jewish Girlz*,

performed in 2002–2003 at the Jewish Community Center, New York (New York: Samuel French, 2005)

At the end of a rehearsal, I often gather the group together and we talk. Although the tone is relaxed, there's still the feeling that this is part of the work. We go around the circle, with each person speaking for a while, presenting stories and ideas that relate to the theme of the show on which we are or will be working. I gently stop any student who goes on too long or who starts to take his monologue into an area that is too difficult emotionally. This isn't censorship—it's editing. To maintain a safe and complex way of working, I want the student to know he or she doesn't have to be emotionally stripped to the bone in order to contribute to the process. I have found, without exception, that in this atmosphere students will speak more openly. The idea is that during these discussions we are mining for information that we can use in the work. I find it appropriate to ask the students to keep these "conversations" confidential. I ask for confidentiality to protect the content of the show, as I want it to remain surprising to our audiences.

After a period of time, I'll ask the students to go off and write a story, monologue, or scene that directly reflects or repeats our discussions. I don't emphasize writing techniques, as such; my hope is that the students will treat writing exercises as storytelling put on paper. My students always read their texts to one another because I emphasize the difference between writing for reading and writing to be said out loud. Some students will take a longer time than others to be comfortable with actually writing down thoughts, characters, and stories. So in the beginning, I ask them to use the exercise as a way to discover how they can capture a moment and then repeat it more than once.

Every group—whether they are making a show on an aspect of their lives or about a Grimm's fairy tale—should come back to a discussion about the news from all over the world. I tell them to report what is happening in a manner that's detailed and engaged. It's important to bring the facts to life. And that can include gossip. The material, political, and spiritual status of your world should be a part of what is considered when making or writing a piece. This is where we live; the world around us influences our reactions and opinions.

While preparing a report on what's going on in the country, culture, or world is a good way to teach the student to do research, be aware that a wide-open shouting match about politics is not necessary (unless your piece happens to be about politics).

Current Events Exercises

Exercise 6.1: Let's talk about what happened in the world today that was interesting or exciting for you.

Aim: To heighten awareness of our large and complex world.

Examples:

1. A bomb went off in Iraq in the green zone.
2. Brad and Angelina were seen together.
3. The elderly are worried about the price of drugs.
4. The Lakers won their third game even without Kobe Bryant.

Aim: To encourage empathy and introduce the causes of global sickness and destruction.

Exercise 6.2: Let's talk about a crisis in the world that was tragic or distressing.

1. The tsunami
2. A drought in Brazil
3. A new kind of flu that's resistant to vaccine

Aim: To break up the solemn mood that world news can bring into the room, and to look for details in the news that aren't immediately apparent, find the ridiculous.

Exercise 6.3: Let's talk about what happened in the world today that was ridiculous or stupid.

1. A man in Detroit ate 125 hot dogs.
2. Ben Stiller threatened to drop out of a movie if there weren't M&M's in his trailer.
3. The Pentagon said that armored trucks weren't better than the ones the soldiers in Iraq have now.
4. An ice sculpture shown at the University of Northern Minnesota melted before the opening.

Aim: To explore news that is hopeful.

Exercise 6.4: Let's talk about what happened in our country, or the world, that was wonderful!

1. They separated the Filipino Siamese twins.
2. They found a whole new set of ancient scrolls.
3. They discovered a new drug to treat Parkinson's disease.
4. The Boston Red Sox won the World Series.

Aim: To explore form and presentation of news by the media.

Exercise 6.5: If spontaneous conversations don't yield facts, the students should go home and find an item from the news, TV, or Internet that catches their attention. Work on a way to present it clearly.

Aim: To learn how to adapt real circumstances to fictional ones.

Exercise 6.6: Go home and find a news item and discuss how you think the individuals in it could be transformed into theatrical characters.

1. Prince Harry and his Nazi jacket, stuck up and spoiled
2. The coal miners who died in West Virginia
3. The brothers who killed their parents because they abused them
4. Angelina Jolie in Africa
5. Nelson Mandela speaking to elementary school children in Seattle

Aim: To encourage active, empathetic thinking; to imagine what having power would be like.

Exercise 6.7: Go home and find an event in the news that you'd most like to change.

1. I'd like the landslide in L.A. to never have happened.
2. I'd like that boy with the toy gun not to have been shot.
3. I'd like the eighty-year-old lady not to have been raped.
4. I'd like for North Korea to get rid of its nuclear weapons.

Aim: To pay attention to stories you don't fully understand and research the rest of the information; to encourage students to ask questions.

Exercise 6.8: Bring in and discuss an item of news that was confusing.

1. I don't know which country is which in Africa.
2. I don't understand who's asking for what in the Middle East.
3. If there's a terror attack, what are we really supposed to do?

Aim: To observe gesture, vocal tone, and posture; to be able to see prominent figures as human beings; to increase perception.

Exercise 6.9: Bring in and discuss a personality in the news whom you admire, don't trust, or think is funny. The other students can agree or disagree.

STUDENT: George Bush—he's forceful and seems nice.

STUDENT: I don't trust him. He smirks.

STUDENT: I like Ted Koppel—his hair looks like Alfred E. Neuman's.

STUDENT: I don't know who he is.

STUDENT: Michael Jackson—I feel sorry for him.

STUDENT: He's disgusting, he sleeps with children.

STUDENT: Condoleezza Rice—she's worked her way up from nothing.

STUDENT: She's cold.

STUDENT: I admire the nurses who work with amputees.

STUDENT: Why are there so many?

STUDENT: Bono is always there for the right cause.

STUDENT: He just does it to get more famous.

Aim: To humanize celebrities; to perceive the people you see every day in a new light; to increase observation.

Exercise 6.10: Bring in and discuss a character in the news that reminds you most of a relative, friend, or acquaintance.

1. Hillary Clinton reminds me of my seventh-grade science teacher: bossy but nice.

2. John Kerry reminds me of my uncle Ted: serious, shy, and tall.

3. Dave Chapelle reminds me of my friend Bart. Funny, but always in trouble.

Aim: To perceive and be moved by something unfamiliar; to broaden vocabulary and experience; to share information cleverly and simply.

Exercise 6.11: Bring in and discuss an event in the news that can teach the group something. What can it teach us?

1. 9/11—people are capable of being good, of helping one another in horrible times.

2. The same with the tsunami.

3. I read about a rabbi and a Muslim cleric who were on tour together talking about peace.

4. A man left all his money to his newspaper boy.

Aim: To observe day-to-day events and transform them into theatrical images.

Exercise 6.12: Bring in and discuss an event in the news that could be made into a play or movie. Why this event? How would you do it?

Example: A congressman is stealing money from his campaign funds. He buys a huge house, a big car. He gets a big head and steals more and more. The press follows the story. The FBI investigates. He gets away with it until . . .

Aim: To encourage the observation of yourself in relation to news events.

Exercise 6.13: Bring in and discuss the event in the news that moved you the most. Why did it move you so much?

1. On *Animal Planet,* all those beached whales that they couldn't save in Massachusetts
2. The girl who got lost in Aruba and just disappeared
3. The woman who lost three sons in Iraq
4. The baby found in the garbage can
5. The student who had to work at three jobs to pay for his college education and started dealing drugs and got killed

I ALTERNATE DISCUSSIONS with storytelling. A story should have a beginning, middle, and end. Most stories have a point of conflict that is either resolved or remains unsolved at the end. In these complicated and confusing times, a linear storytelling structure might not be your choice of style, but the director should encourage storytelling nonetheless, although the form can vary. If a play works, each moment within the whole has its own story—its own beginning, middle, and end. Furthermore, you have a deeper understanding of an isolated event as it happens in the context of a story. Your reflections go beyond simple opinions. You see more than one side and start to understand that the misuse of power or the abuse of people could be bound up in seemingly unrelated circumstance. You learn to use metaphor and different voices to enlarge your story.

General Storytelling Exercises

Ask each student to go home and prepare to tell a story.

Aim: To recognize what pride is, and when you felt it; to add a strong, positive emotion to your vocabulary by revisiting a moment of strength and self-esteem.

Exercise 6.14: Talk about a time when you felt the most proud.

Examples:

1. When my dad caught a huge bass. We were in this little boat, in the middle of this huge lake. And the two of us were just sitting there talking about how quiet it was, when this huge fish pulled so hard on my father's line, he almost went in. And so I grabbed hold of his leg and he started fighting with the fish like it was a dance—pulling, being pulled, giving him line, yanking him in real close. My dad was so cool about it, you know, so focused. And finally after half an hour, he got the sucker. That fish had to weigh twenty-five pounds and would've been a real trophy, but my dad threw him back in the water because he'd been such a "noble fighter." Of course no one believed us. But I knew.

2. When I aced the math final

3. The first time I skated backward

4. When my first article was published in the school paper

5. When I took on Suzi Mayser

6. When I'd hung out with the Lords (or someone else)

Aim: To learn that you are not alone when you mess up; to detoxify mistakes by making them funny. Also, many good stories are based on mistakes or embarrassments.

Exercise 6.15: Talk about a time when you embarrassed yourself.

1. My mom (or someone) embarrasses me when she rubs food off my chin with her thumb.

2. Last week my pants almost fell down in the hallway.

3. I was crying in the bathroom and Mrs. Driscoll came in.

4. This huge guy went to hit me and I ran, I just ran.

Aim: To take time to reevaluate your own definition of real courage.

Exercise 6.16: Talk about an act that you thought was truly courageous, in your life or in the world.

1. My dad jumped into the street and yanked my little sister out of the way of a speeding car.

2. I think the soldiers in Iraq are courageous.

3. I think my friend Jaime was courageous when she switched gangs.

4. Randy got onstage and sang with laryngitis.

Aim: To once again relive a time when you saw yourself as strong.

Exercise 6.17: When do you think you were the most courageous? Do you feel that way now?

1. When I told my parents I'd been smoking / I used drugs / I was gay

2. When I refused to do meth and my friends mocked me

3. When I made it through initiation

4. When I stood up to my father

Aim: To redefine what it means to be a coward and to lessen the humiliation stemming from what you did or didn't do.

Exercise 6.18: When were you the most cowardly?

1. When I didn't ask Michelle J. out
2. When a plane I was on started bumping and I screamed
3. When I just watched my dad beat up my mom
4. When I didn't get tested
5. When I agreed to throw rocks at the cars and then ran

AFTER A SUFFICIENT NUMBER of questions and answers, let the group get up and do some movement exercises or improvs. Then call it a day. If you extend a complicated discussion past a reasonable time, the students will get tired and start to feel as though it's all the same and they won't be as thorough and excited about their assignments as they should be.

HERE ARE some more exercises to encourage storytelling.

Aim: To explore suspense, shared secrets, and the lies in which adolescents specialize.

Exercise 6.19: Tell a story about the time you or someone else got away with something (a minor incident or real crime).

1. I went out with this boy and told my parents I was sleeping at my friend's house.
2. I think Robert Blake got away with murder.

Aim: To create a story in which the lead character will face consequences.

Exercise 6.20: Talk about yourself or someone else getting caught.

1. My friend Sam was caught stealing cash out of his brother's wallet.
2. I had a condom in my wallet that Mom found when she was cleaning.

Aim: To compare the techniques parents use and see which are the worst or the most original.

Exercise 6.21: How are you punished? How are friends punished?

1. TV goes off, computer off, no games, no phone, I'm grounded.
2. My friend Jake got hit with his father's belt.

Aim: To look deeply into a word that is taken for granted and find more than the meaning.

Exercise 6.22: What is punishment?

Aim: To continue to explore the notion of justice.

Exercise 6.23: Who is punished fairly or unfairly?

1. Me sometimes. When I lie about being at school.
2. Unfairly—when I get hit if I don't know what I did.
3. Too harshly—those Arabs in Iraq.
4. Not harshly enough—my cousin—he took his dad's car out, bashed a fender, and wasn't even grounded.
5. I wish there was a punishment for when a friend drops you.

Aim: To explore the many definitions of gift; to explore positive relationships.

Exercise 6.24: Talk about a great gift you or someone you know received.

1. I didn't hand in the paper, but the teacher gave me another week.
2. This T-shirt
3. My mom
4. A free burger after school
5. A car

Aim: To explore the many forms of generosity and to present yourself in a truly positive light.

Exercise 6.25: Talk about a great gift you or someone else gave.

1. I gave my girlfriend this gold heart for Valentine's Day.
2. I gave my mom me!
3. I wrote a poem for Sam.
4. I cleaned my room.

Exercise 6.26: When have you been generous?

1. I bought my best friend a CD.
2. I always give my brother the bottom part of my ice cream cone (he likes it best).
3. I gave Tina my science notes.
4. I stand up for Cyndi because girls pick on her.
5. I taught Jim some guitar chords.

6. I wash the dishes.

7. I was nice to Tim even though he's not one of the cool ones.

Aim: To learn aspects of basic human nature that are less than angelic and that are typical but unpleasant.

Exercise 6.27: When have you been selfish or stingy?

1. When I wouldn't share my pizza

2. When I wouldn't lend Marcy my skirt

3. When I wouldn't tell Eliza what me and the girls were talking about

4. When I wouldn't go out with John to his cousin's place

5. When I complained about how I was bored at home when Dad was sick

Aim: To describe aspects of selfishness as they affect you.

Exercise 6.28: Whom do you know who is selfish or stingy, and why?

1. My mother can be so selfish. I gotta squeeze every penny outta her.

2. My friend Alex—he never lets me ride his bike.

3. My dad says my uncle Tim has never once paid the check.

Aim: To explore consequences or the lack thereof.

Exercise 6.29: What did your selfishness lead to?

1. Being alone

2. Fights

3. Getting the cold shoulder

Aim: To foster an understanding of how small human failings can build into the actions of leaders and powerful groups.

Exercise 6.30: What does extreme selfishness lead to?

1. Fights, anger, people going after the selfish person.
2. Like Tim—he would not let us look at his cards. He was really stupid, so we held him down and took them from him.

Aim: To recognize and reveal what is irrational.

Exercise 6.31: Describe selfishness that is ridiculous.

1. Over a corner of the block: "This is *my* corner." "No, this is *my* corner."
2. He's *my* friend. Stay away.
3. I told you not to touch that piece of cake.

Aim: To follow how a simple disagreement can develop into a confrontation.

Exercise 6.32: Describe a time when you've seen two or three people fight over:

1. A material thing
   a. Me and my sister over a brush
2. A way of doing things
   a. How to be a parent
   b. Riding a bike
   c. Playing a game
   d. How much my mom says she knows my dad can drink
   e. My dad saying my mom's stupid

3. A rumor (true or not)

    a. Sally Rae pushing Tina because someone said that Tina was spreading the rumor that Sally Rae "did it" with Larry Johnson

    b. Michael telling everyone that Jean has to go to fat kids' camp. She's humiliated.

4. An accusation

    a. My brother says I leave the bathroom a mess, I say *he* does.

    b. He tried to take my backpack, so I kicked him.

    c. Sam thought that Mark was looking at him in a "funny way." Mark said Sam was crazy.

    d. My grandma thought I stole her hidden cash.

5. The attention of another person

    a. Mark really beat that new Kevin guy up to show us how to treat outsiders.

    b. Mike kicked Jay so Sally would see how tough he was.

    c. I stopped eating so my mother would freak out.

Aim: To observe and record, in an objective way, something that is usually very emotional; to expand the vocabulary and motivation of movement.

Exercise 6.33: Describe different ways in which humans fight; put specific words to each form. Then write a description of a fight between two people.

1. Yelling

2. Calling names

3. Hitting

4. Using weapons

5. Withholding material things

6. Mocking each other, putting each other down

7. Giving the cold shoulder

8. Getting the other person in trouble

Aim: To explore words for clearly depicting something sudden and shocking.

Exercise 6.34: Describe the worst fight you've ever seen.

1. My father got in the car and went about ninety down the street. My mother wanted him to give her the keys.

2. Some skinheads came into the Korean deli with baseball bats. The owner pulled a knife.

Aim: To be able to give a comedic interpretation to confrontations.

Exercise 6.35: Describe a ridiculous fight you or someone you know fought.

1. Me and my sister practically soaked each other with face creams and conditioner and liquid soap over who got to use the shower.

2. My mom and dad stopped talking to each other because she said Uncle Ralph was cheap, and my father said Uncle Ralph was shy. We had to talk for them all week.

Exercise 6.36: What causes people to "choose sides"? Talk about when you had to choose a side.

Note: Now that you have the idea, you can ask questions within a theme to deepen the students' understanding of a topic and therefore help them to think in more complete ways.

Aim: To personalize universal experiences; to explore the various outcomes of fights. How does the "music" go? Are the consonants sharp? Do the fighters speak quickly or slowly, loudly or softly? Do the fighters talk at the same time?

Exercise 6.37: Talk about a time you or someone you know was in the middle of a fight. How do fights grow? Into what do they grow? Why? Who benefits from a fight?

Exercise 6.38: Describe a time when you saw or participated in a fight that was easily resolved. How? Why?

Exercise 6.39: Talk about how you or someone you know resolved a fight. How did he or she do it? Who benefited from the outcome?

Storytelling Exercises About Relationships

Aim: To find personal expression for a very general state of being by using the story and details of one person's experience.

Exercise 6.40: Have you or anyone you know ever been in love? (Don't try to define it—go with your gut.) Was this person uninterested, or were you loved in return?

Aim: To make detailed observations about emotions, behavior, and feelings.

Exercise 6.41: How was that love expressed?

1. Describe a form of expression you heard about (or used) that was over the top or ridiculous.

2. Describe a moment when you or someone you know was unable to express love.

Exercise 6.42: Was it a good or bad kind of love? Why?

Exercise 6.43: Describe when you and someone else met for the first time. What was funny about it? What was romantic?

Aim: To learn to talk about emotions and feelings in detail.

Exercise 6.44: Describe the love you or someone you know experiences in close friendships.

Exercise 6.45: How is it expressed? Describe an act of friendship of a friend or someone else's friend that is interesting or funny to you.

Exercise 6.46: How does a friendship evolve? Talk about how you became friends with someone over time. What did you and your friend share? Adventures? Opinions? Choices of food, music, clothing?

Exercise 6.47: Describe a serious fight with a friend. Describe a humorous fight. How did you make up?

Aim: To describe in detail what is usually a nonverbal event.

Exercise 6.48: Talk about a time when you felt that your father or mother truly loved you. Why? When?

Exercise 6.49: Talk about a time you felt real love for your mother or father (or both). What did they do or not do? What did they say or not say?

Aim: To observe the shift in language, tone, and feeling when unpleasant emotions are described.

Exercise 6.50: Describe a moment when you hated a parent. What caused your feelings? What happened? What did she or he do?

Aim: To give words and visualizations to an unspoken moment of emotion.

Exercise 6.51: Describe a time when your father or mother seemed to hate you. Why? What did you do or not do? Say or not say?

Aim: To recognize states of feeling that are often taken for granted.

Exercise 6.52: Describe a time when you felt this way about your family—and why:

1. Ashamed
2. Proud
3. Bored

Aim: To learn to use every connection as a source for material.

Exercise 6.53: What about your siblings—your cousins?

1. When have you been close?
2. When have you hated them?
3. What happened?

Aim: To describe an event without generalizing.

Exercise 6.54: Describe a holiday with your family that was pleasant or fun. Where? With whom? What made it pleasant?

Aim: To describe an event and perceive what caused a change in atmosphere during it.

Exercise 6.55: Describe a holiday that was a disappointment or disaster for your family. Who ruined it? What did they do?

Aim: To study people you take for granted as characters.

Exercise 6.56: Describe a relative.
1. The craziest
2. The one you know least
3. The one who's your friend

Aim: To examine former states of mind that were vivid but now feel different.

Exercise 6.57: Have you ever wanted to run away? Why? To where?

Exercise 6.58: Describe your plans when you wanted to run away.
1. How were you going to live?
2. What's the happy ending in your imagination?
3. What's the unhappy ending?

Aim: To learn how to gather information in order to expand your vocabulary of "moments" for your storytelling.

Exercise 6.59: Have you ever heard about other students who . . .

1. left home?
2. used drugs?
3. were hookers?
4. were promiscuous?
5. were dangerous?
6. were bad tempered?
7. were impatient?
8. received honors?
9. helped others?
10. were funny?
11. worked an after-school job?
12. were patient?
13. were easygoing?
14. were talented at something?

Aim: To examine objectively and in detail an event that, at the time, didn't involve words.

Exercise 6.60: Describe a time when you felt real fear.

1. What happened?
2. How did it feel?
3. Did you get over it?
4. How?

Aim: To observe the characteristics of extreme behavior and to call up your reactions to it.

Exercise 6.61: Describe the angriest person you've ever seen.

1. Did he or she scare you?
2. Make you laugh?
3. Make you sorry?

Aim: To balance negative observations with specific moments of real delight.

Exercise 6.62: Describe a moment that felt truly wonderful.

1. What happened?
2. Where was it?
3. Who was involved?

Exercise 6.63: Describe a moment when you felt awful.

Aim: To distinguish the extreme from the ordinary and be able to express it.

Exercise 6.64: What is the strangest or most awful secret you or someone you know has had to keep?

Aim: To redefine what is heroic and what is not in a character's actions.

Exercise 6.65: Describe a time when you or a person you know lied to protect you or someone else.

Personalizing Classic Stories

If you notice, these questions have to be answered *specifically* with regard to time, descriptions, and remembrance of participants and events. It is this specificity that will ultimately help you and your students write performable poems, monologues, scenes, and songs.

The same method can be used for interpreting fairy tales and myths. For instance, let's take the Hans Christian Andersen tale "The Emperor's New Clothes."

Aim: To give detail and truth to a broad character; to observe the details of someone's clothes; to see why they seem one way to them and another way to you.

Exercise 6.66: Talk about yourself or a person who is crazy about clothes.

1. What kind of clothes?
2. Does he or she like whole outfits or just like shoes, hats, jeans, dresses?

Exercise 6.67: Discuss how this person (or you) walks when he/she is wearing something "fabulous."

Aim: To continue to observe different behavior from every aspect.

Exercise 6.68: Discuss why clothes matter so much to this person or to you.

Aim: To understand political or psychological reasons behind a character choice.

Exercise 6.69: The Emperor values clothes more than anything. Talk about a person you know who values material things above all else. Why?

Aim: To probe the deeper message of the tale.

Exercise 6.70: Talk about why you or your friends try to impress each other or a specific time you saw or heard this happening.

1. Was it funny?
2. Was it annoying?
3. Did it make you nervous?

Aim: To explore and identify a class of people that is foreign to you.

Exercise 6.71: The Emperor can have any clothes he wants from all over the world. Do you know someone who is incredibly rich? Have you read about such a person?

1. How does he spend the money?
2. What privileges does he get?

Aim: To observe a class of people as characters and determine what makes them similar; to see your own prejudices.

Exercise 6.72: How are rich people interesting? How are they boring? Talk about a time when you (or someone you know) had these specific feelings about the very rich:

1. Jealousy
2. Disgust
3. Awe

Aim: To explore aspects of the Emperor's weakness in yourself and others.

Exercise 6.73: Talk about a dream you or someone you know had about being rich.

Aim: To use the Emperor as a jumping-off point for discovering similar behavior in others.

Exercise 6.74: The Emperor is supposed to be ruling the land. Talk about a leader or celebrity in our country or another who is corrupt.

1. Takes money away from the poor
2. Pretends to be feeling a certain way
3. Is famous but also a criminal

4. Doesn't care about anyone but himself

5. Is lazy

Aim: To compare the earlier discussions about the world with this fictional one.

Exercise 6.75: The Emperor is so self-involved he couldn't care less about his people. Discuss the same corruption or hypocrisy in your life and talk about a person close to you who you think abuses power or popularity.

1. A parent

2. A principal or teacher

3. A popular athlete

4. A coach

5. A star student

6. The leader of a clique or gang

Aim: To think about personal solutions to this story.

Exercise 6.76: The reader can see the Emperor is a fool. How can this person be exposed?

Aim: To find humorous behavior in broad fairy-tale characters.

Exercise 6.77: The tailors arrive. They sell their invaluable cloth. Talk about a famous person who is a prankster or practical joker.

Aim: To observe in detail how one person can manipulate another with the use of the powers of imagination (even if they are sometimes cruel).

Exercise 6.78: Talk about someone you know who plays tricks on others.

1. What kind of tricks?

2. On whom?

3. Why?

Aim: To find similarities between current events and a fairy tale.

Exercise 6.79: Talk about a crime you've heard of in which someone embezzled money, cheated with stocks, fixed numbers in a company's records, or lied about who they were and what they did.

1. Who cheated?

2. What did they do?

Exercise 6.80: The Emperor falls for the tailors' scam. Talk about a person you know who is gullible. What makes someone gullible?

Aim: To make the story relevant to your own life.

Exercise 6.81: The tailors pretend to work hard on the Emperor's clothes. Talk about how you or someone you know similarly carried on a fake drama to get their own way.

1. Faking being sick

2. Faking having a boyfriend or girlfriend

3. Faking being in one place when actually you're in another

4. Faking working hard when you're not

5. Making up a story to cover your own tracks

Aim: To examine peer pressure as part of a broad characterization and then from a more personal perspective.

Exercise 6.82: The Emperor's courtiers pretend they see the fabulous clothes because they're afraid of being called stupid. Talk about a time when peer pressure swayed you or a friend to do something foolish.

1. You did something dangerous or wrong.
2. You dressed or talked a certain way.
3. You pretended to know more than you did.
4. You excluded others.
5. You went against common sense.

Aim: To once again see how a great fairy tale can reflect the present; to observe world politics with a critical eye.

Exercise 6.83: The Emperor shows his new clothes to the public, but he is actually naked. Still, the citizens pretend to see the clothes. Talk about an event in the news or in your city where people were transformed into a mob or crowd.

Exercise 6.84: Talk about a time when you or someone you know has made a fool of himself in public.

Aim: To discuss the part of human nature that makes us try to hide our limitations.

Exercise 6.85: Talk about a time when you or someone you know got caught being phony.

1. Lying
2. Not knowing an answer
3. Pretending a fall didn't hurt
4. Talking in a phony accent

Aim: To use the story of the Emperor's new clothes as a jumping-off point for self-examination as well as political history.

Exercise 6.86: Why won't most people question authority?

Aim: To identify and describe a person with candor.

Exercise 6.87: In the tale, only a child dares to cry out, "He has no clothes on." Who is the most honest person you know? Why?

Aim: To explore the drawbacks of honesty.

Exercise 6.88: Talk about a time when you or someone you know had to be honest, even when it meant causing pain or trouble.

Aim: To observe a kid or group of kids in a new way, without resorting to stereotypes.

Exercise 6.89: Talk about a person much younger than you who has spontaneous, honest reactions.

Aim: To discuss how elements such as upbringing and outside influences can create character.

Exercise 6.90: What would make a person more truthful?

THOROUGH QUESTIONS and answers can evolve into conversations and help a student create a character. Whether you are creating an original piece or adapting an existing story, the student should become as "fluent" as possible in the entire universe of your subject.

If you are creating an issue-oriented piece, you can tailor your questions around the specific subject.

Discussing Appearances

Aim: To examine definitions and stereotypes; to explore personal taste.

Exercise 6.91: Who do you think is the most physically beautiful person in the world?

1. Bring in pictures and explain.
2. Describe this person if you have no picture.

Aim: To counteract stereotypical thinking and recognize character attributes rather than just physical characteristics.

Exercise 6.92: Talk about someone you know or have seen who has moved you or got your respect in spite of their looks (or because of attributes other than physical beauty).

Aim: To explore how our opinions are affected by what's in media and popular culture.

Exercise 6.93: In our society what makes a person "beautiful"?

1. Body
2. Face

3. Clothes

4. Walk

Aim: To address the reality that good looks create power.

Exercise 6.94: Describe someone who is popular because of their looks.

Aim: To examine the value contemporary society puts on beauty.

Exercise 6.95: Why does beauty matter?

Aim: To examine the definition of beauty presented by the media.

Exercise 6.96: What images of beauty (or coolness) do you get through the following media:

1. Magazines

2. TV

3. Movies/videos/DVDs

Aim: To look at yourself in a new, objective way.

Exercise 6.97: How do you and your friends try to replicate that kind of look?

1. Clothes

2. Accessories

3. Ways of standing, talking

4. Hair

Aim: To encourage an exploration of how styles change.

Exercise 6.98: Describe some old styles; then identify some new ones.

Aim: To encourage objective observation.

Exercise 6.99: Name a group in school whose members dress alike. Consider cliques, age groups, gangs.

Aim: To think about your peers and try to see them objectively.

Exercise 6.100: Why do members of groups dress alike?

Aim: To use imagination and research skills.

Exercise 6.101: How do you think fashions and fads come to be?

Aim: To recognize the psychological aspects of some stylistic choices.

Exercise 6.102: Describe someone you know or have seen who *purposely* dresses differently.
  1. What kind of reaction does this person get?
  2. What do you think this person wants?

Aim: To examine and define "the other."

Exercise 6.103: Describe a person who doesn't know that he or she is "out of it." Why does such a person end up dressing or looking that way?

Aim: To get in touch with your empathetic side and possibly resolve your own discomfort with mirrors.

Exercise 6.104: Improvise or write a monologue from the point of view of someone looking in a mirror and not liking what he or she sees.

Aim: To identify the characteristics of positive self-esteem.

Exercise 6.105: Describe someone who likes his or her outer image.

Aim: To recognize arrogance.

Exercise 6.106: Describe someone who likes himself or herself too much.

Aim: To look deeply at your peers or parents and think about their unhappiness.

Exercise 6.107: Describe someone you know who hates herself or himself.

1. Why do you think he or she feels this way?
2. How does this self-hatred manifest itself?

Aim: To introduce the issue of eating disorders.

Exercise 6.108: Think of someone who is too fat (or too thin).

1. What kind of clothes does he or she wear?
2. What kind of personality does this person have?
3. How did he or she come to be overweight (or underweight)?

Aim: To examine what is healthy and what is not.

Exercise 6.109: Describe what some of your friends do to stay thin.

1. Work out
2. Diet
3. Fast
4. Eating dos or don'ts

Aim: To explore your own taste and imagination.

Exercise 6.110: Invent your own fad diet.

Exercise 6.111: Invent your own line of fashion and accessories and put on a show.

Exercise 6.112: Invent a uniform for you and your friends.

Aim: To explore issues of conformity and difference.

Exercise 6.113: How does wearing a uniform or similar clothes every day affect or not affect daily life?

Aim: To explore the value of individual expression and its consequences.

Exercise 6.114: Imagine a world where everyone dressed the same. What do they look like? What is this world like?

Aim: To acquaint yourself with those who hate or fear "the other."

Exercise 6.115: Create a character who despises others who are different.

1. In dress
2. In size
3. In attitude
4. In color

Aim: To explore the roots of prejudice.

Exercise 6.116: What would make one person despise another because of his or her appearance? Create such a character. Does he or she feel:

1. Afraid: why?
2. Angry: why?
3. Superior: why?
4. Inferior: why?

Aim: To explore how prejudice and fear can lead to confrontation.

Exercise 6.117: Describe two individuals who have a conflict because they look or act differently. Do the same with two groups.

Aim: To examine how prejudice is passed on.

Exercise 6.118: Think of how feelings of suspicion and dislike of "others" come to be.

1. Taught by parents
2. Encouraged by school or government
3. Reaction to a specific bad experience
4. Rumors

Aim: To examine the danger of faulty information and intentional lying.

Exercise 6.119: Create a bizarre rumor about someone who looks or acts different (a small rumor, then a bigger and bigger one).

1. How do rumors grow and change?
2. Why do people believe in them?

Aim: To identify a person who has deep prejudice.

Exercise 6.120: Create a character who tells lies about someone who is different from him or her.

1. What are the lies?
2. Why does the character tell them?
3. Why do people believe the character?

Aim: To examine the possibility of change in human nature.

Exercise 6.121: Describe or create a situation in which two very different people learn to accept their differences. How and why does this happen?

Aim: To examine truthfulness and its consequences.

Exercise 6.122: Describe a situation in which rumors about someone prove to be wrong.

1. How does such a situation come about?
2. What are the reactions of the people involved?

Aim: To understand how the small fears and prejudices of individuals can be blown up into events that can affect the state of the world.

Exercise **6.123:** Describe a historical event or a current event that took place because two individuals or groups were different.

REMEMBER: any of these descriptions, stories, or events can be fictional, half true, or fact-based. The material ranges from personal to psychological to societal to political and back again. No question or answer is more significant or weighty than any other, because by not defining what is "important" or "not important," the student may discover that a small detail or a description of a trivial character may end up being more revealing than a larger generalization.

MORE THEMES FOR DISCUSSION

Aim: To use what you have learned to discuss a chosen topic and to switch fluidly from topic to topic. The suggested major subjects are followed by specific areas for possible in-depth discussion.

1. Family. Explore jealousy, abuse, companionship, all manner of relationships.

2. Loss. Explore reasons for grief, good and bad ways of coping.

3. Sports. Explore competition, violence, pride, feelings of inferiority, the joy of using the body, the disparity between great athletes and their behavior.

4. Weekends. Explore what "play" is, how to have fun, why weekends are an oasis, why they can be dreaded, descriptions of car rides with family, parties, dating.

5. Creative pursuits (theater, painting, music, and so on). Explore the joy of self-expression, how writing or painting or acting can help soothe you or give you confidence (or the opposite).

6. Friends. Discuss stories of loyalty, betrayal, depictions of what you and your friends do, what you expect of one another.

7. Food. Examine diet, tastes, love of eating, what food reveals about people, eating disorders, food binges, fasting.

8. Violence. Relate stories or depictions of personal experiences with violence, testimonies of witnessing or reading about violence, violence done to you or a friend, what stops violence, what makes a person go over the line, what the roots of violence are, where those roots are apparent in friends, family, one another, how violence gets passed down through a family or among friends.

9. Racism. Discuss experiences of difference, behavior toward "the other," defining who's different from whom, individual stories, experiences that illustrate racism, ways in which a relative expresses racism, the possibility of eliminating racism.

10. Honor. Discuss when someone behaved honorably or dishonorably; why a close friend or classmate feels that he or she must defend his or her honor.

11. Poor versus rich. Look at who is poor and who is rich in your life and in the world. How do they act?

12. Fear. Explore what you are afraid of. What scared you when you were young? What have you seen friends or family do when afraid? How have you seen fear exploited? How do you express fear?

13. Sex. Explore interest in sex, fear of sex, guilt over sex, the dangers of sex, disgust about sex, longing for sex, warnings about disease and pregnancy.

14. Drug use. Discuss specific drugs and their dangers and why friends become addicted. Do you know pushers? Users? Have you done drugs? What did they do? What do you see happening to friends who are constantly using drugs? Why does the story always end badly? Are drugs ever helpful to you? To your friends? Discuss prescription drugs, ADD, ADHD, and how all

these can create changes in perception, time, space. (ADD and ADHD are attention deficit disorders which affect a person's ability to concentrate or remain still.)

15. Health. Discuss what a healthy lifestyle is—and how fast food, exercise, laziness, carelessness, smoking, drink, sleep, lack of sleep, having protected sex do or do not play a part in it.

16. Abuse. Discuss what abuse is. Do you know someone who has been abused? Have you? If so, what kind of abuse?

17. Insanity. When do you feel as if you're going crazy? When has someone around you started acting strange—too happy or too sad? What makes someone mentally ill?

18. The streets. Describe the world of the bad streets: drugs, violence, gangs.

19. Differences. Talk about the differences between poor and rich neighborhoods. Why do people of different religions or origins tend to live in isolated groups?

World Topics

1. War. When is war ever necessary? What problems can war solve? What are the issues behind wars?

2. The military. How would you feel if you were drafted? What's good about the military? Bad?

3. HIV. Talk about HIV and AIDS. These diseases attack the immune system and can result from having unprotected sex. Describe symptoms and treatments as well as their effect on life in both America and Africa. If you get AIDS, you might die. If you are HIV-positive, you have to take a lot of medicines every day. Talk about how HIV and AIDS are destroying the population in Africa because there are not enough drugs

available. Why do people spread such lethal diseases? What are the symptoms of AIDS? Who do you know who has it? Have you known anyone who died from it?

4. Prison. Explore what it's like to be inside a prison. Do you know someone who has been incarcerated? Is prison good or bad for offenders? Why? What kind of people go to prison? Commit crimes? Are some innocent?

5. Environment. Think about the air, the sea, the city. What's the most polluted place you have ever been? What do you think can be done to save oceans, rivers, lakes, forests? What is global warming? Why should you care? Is our weather changing?

6. Space. Discuss where in the universe you think we will be exploring in the next one hundred years. Would you like to live in space?

7. Religion. Discuss how different religions worship. What do they each believe in? How do different religions practice? What is good about faith? What is dangerous? Why do so many people go to war in the name of God? What do you believe? Have you ever been intolerant?

8. Terrorism. Discuss the possible effects of terrorism. Are you frightened of what might happen? What are terrorists? What groups do they belong to and represent? Why do they do what they do? What do you think can stop terrorism? What should be done to prevent it?

9. Media. Discuss what you hear on the news. Do you believe it? What channels do you watch? What do you think of journalists? Who's real? Who's phony? Do the media have too much influence on your generation? In what ways are the media important?

10. Current events. Discuss what happened in the world today, this week, this year? What happened in our city, our state, our country? Relate other people's stories, stories that inspire, facts that infuriate you.

Relationships

1. Dating, flirting, and love. Talk about the relationships between young men and women. Who has more power? Who makes the decisions? What makes a good relationship? Describe a terrible relationship you had. Describe a good one. How do you know when you're in love? What is the best way to express love? What is wrong with cheating? What's good about freedom? How do you let someone know you're interested in him or her? Describe your own ways of flirting. Describe a friend's way of flirting. What should you do on a date? What's fun? Describe a good date and a bad one. Who gets the best girls or guys? What does that mean? What kind of person impresses you? Describe an ideal boyfriend/girlfriend. Explain why you are happy/unhappy with the boyfriend/girlfriend you have now. Why are some kids popular and others not? Talk about friendships among girls; among guys. Do they talk about love? Where do parents influence and fit into your social life? Finally, talk about coming out if you are gay or a story about someone you know who came out. What were the consequences or rewards?

2. Boyfriend or girlfriend jealousies, disagreements, cheating, breakups.

3. Meeting new loves. Discuss seeing someone with whom you become enraptured; talking to someone and finding you agree on everything; playing a sport with (or against) someone and finding you fall in love. Or talk about dancing together, being lab partners, or both sitting shyly in a corner at a party.

Note: I avoid talking about specific acts of sex or descriptions of the body. I think that no matter how sophisticated the kids may be, they don't want to dwell on the topic of sex while an adult is present, even in sex ed class, when they *have* to. I do, however, discuss teenage pregnancy, AIDS, and STDs if it seems appropriate to do so.

Lighter Topics

1. Animal conversations. Explore these either in animal language or translated into English.

2. Stories of animals. Talk about your pet, someone else's pet, wild animals, mythological animals, animal rights.

3. Behavior. Discuss mischief, cruelty, generosity, stupidity, and so on. Describe someone who has exhibited a specific sort of behavior. Describe what he or she did—and why. Think about various kinds of behavior: yours and other people's.

4. Myths and fables. Bring in a myth or fable from another country—from the South, the Islands, and so on. What makes something a superstition? How do superstitions come to be?

YOU AND THE STUDENTS should first carry on these discussions in a real-life way, using the student or someone he or she knows as a model. Then you should discuss your chosen topic again, but this time from the point of view of a made-up character.

Example:

Character: a tough, steel-hearted gang member

Q: Who is the person you admire most in the world?

A: Me, who else?

Q: When was a time you felt proud?

A: When I kicked the geek in study hall and he fell off his chair.

Character: a phony head of an exclusive clique

Q: Who is the person you admire most in the world?

A: Paris Hilton.

Q: When was a time you felt proud?

A: The day Susan, Jessica, Ruth, and I sat at a table in the cafeteria and *everyone* wanted to sit with us.

Character: a four-year-old boy who is in the middle of a cowboy battle

Q: Who is the person you admire most in the world?

A: Mommy and Daddy.

Q: When was a time you felt proud?

A: When I sang for Aunt Olga—she's real nice to me. She lets me live with her when Mommy and Daddy are fighting.

SEVEN

WRITING

JOYCE: It's a beautiful but freezing March Friday, and I am in the
elevator, only a few seconds away from collapsing from an
exhaustive week of school. I step out of the elevator and walk
down the hall and can already smell the rich aromas coming
from the kitchen. Shabbat is coming. It's one of my few
indescribable feelings. Come on, a huge delicious meal, and
the only dinner I get to share with my family. As I walk into my
apartment, I rush into the kitchen. I open all the pots to see
what delicious foods await me at dinner. As I look at the foods
not only do I get a tingly feeling in my glands, but also I decide
to pick at all the pots. After I get a taste of the meal, consisting
of Sephardic goodies, yebrat, kiftes, hamid and more, I actually
get a spiritual feeling. Friday. No school for two days, and a
great meal in a couple hours. Who could ask for more?

— Joyce, age fifteen, in *Jewish Girlz*

TONGUE RING

With my tongue ring i can do lots of stuff. When I'm bored I can
play with it. When I annoyd I can play with it. When I'm with my
girlfriend . . . I CAN PLAY WITH IT. I must say ever since I got
this, I gained respect. People respect me b'cause I went through a
"painful" experience. Something a lot of people were scared and
said they'd never do I guess you cansay I've got balls. But in the end
I like 2 say I've got a tonguering

—Vaughn, age sixteen, in *Loss and Gain*

There are thousands of books on how to write, including how to write
in different genres. This chapter presents a group of exercises that I
hope will inspire students to write without frustration, fear, or dislike
of the written word, as well as to experiment with words and emotions, styles and rhythm. There is enormous power in experiencing
the joy of writing work that is your own.

I will also demonstrate different ways of using students' words and
ideas, despite the fact that their writing may not be strong enough to
be included in a final presentation. If original writing is not possible
but you don't want to do a conventional or existing play, you or another teacher can adapt the students' ideas and spontaneous improvs
into a form that truthfully represents the spirit and the students'
words. Thus, this chapter is not about playwriting in the conventional
sense of the word. I am only presenting exercises to inspire writing
that can be included in a work made with and by students as an ensemble, so my emphasis is on storytelling and theatrical journalism.

The results of these exercises may or may not end up being part of
your final work. You should allot time within the given rehearsal period
for students to write on the spot. That is so they can commiserate with
one another, easily ask you questions, or ask for help if they are lost.
Otherwise, writing may feel like homework, even though, to the extent
possible, the writing process should intrigue the student as much as any

other creative endeavor. If a piece works and needs rewriting, I will have the students do it at home. You should also say from the top that if anyone is inspired by the exercises in the room, he or she is welcome to write individually at home. I always find that several students will begin to pour out material and discover themselves as writers.

Note: Depending on the level of reading skill, some students may require extra rehearsal time. When the motives and exchanges become complex, it's important that everyone be able to read fluidly. Cold readings are impossible for students without the right skills, and they discourage the writer as well as the reader.

Once again I'd like to emphasize that even this late in the process, students should not be allowed to critique one another— positively or negatively. First of all, they're not ready to judge objectively. Second, any criticizing of one another will cause the ensemble to deteriorate. I often discourage applause after individual presentations because students are so sensitive that they will be affected by who gets the higher volume or length of applause.

General Writing Exercises

Aim: To begin to understand the relationship between an original voice and content.

Exercise 7.1: Ask your students to go off and write an excuse for why they can't make it to rehearsal tomorrow. Give them five minutes to do this. The piece should be no longer than three minutes and no shorter than two lines. When the students return, ask each to read his or her excuse out loud. I emphasize the importance of hearing the work read out loud. Nonsense, absurdity, and playing with words should be encouraged. I'm not concerned with proper grammar as long as the voice is believable and the image clear.

Example: I'm sorry I can't come tomorrow; I have to take my cat to an eye examination. She's been walking into walls.

SPECIFICITY, as in our other work, should be encouraged. Generalization rarely makes for good writing.

Example: Student reads: I can't go to rehearsal tomorrow because I'm sick and I don't feel well.

Now I'll give the student an "adjustment" or suggestion for a way to create a more interesting and lively version of her excuse.

Adjustment:

LIZ: Great, but sick with what?

STUDENT: A cold.

LIZ: Tell me some symptoms.

STUDENT: I don't know — stuffy nose, sore throat, pimple on my tongue.

LIZ: Okay, so put that in. I'm not going to believe you for one minute unless you really tell me what it feels like. How's your belly?

STUDENT: I got gas.

LIZ: Good. The grosser the better. Do the excuse again and put all that in.

Rewrite: I'm sorry I can't show up, cause I'm sick. I got snot running from my nose and my throat has scabs and my tongue has a zit and I got gas.

In the beginning, if one student comes up with a piece of writing that works, the others may imitate it. In this case, 75 percent of the students will now use the excuse of being sick. If that is the case, I say something like: "It's boring if you are all sick. Think of something else—like you had to rescue a turtle from being cooked or the sidewalk sucked you in and you were kidnapped by an army of ants." I never hesitate to use my own admittedly silly examples to provide assurance that the students can be as imaginative as their minds will let them.

Here is a great excuse one fifteen-year-old girl wrote:

I'm sorry I'm late but my pantyhose fell and got my ankles all tangled up and then the subway caught on fire and I couldn't run because my ankles were all caught up and then a man tried to pick me up and carry me but I'm too heavy so he had a heart attack and the doctors came and they cut my pantyhose so I could run from the subway but I tripped and fell into a homeless person who told me my fortune and said I shouldn't get back on any subway take a bus and the buses were all crowded so I had to wait half an hour.

A more concise excuse from a twelve-year-old boy:

I'm sorry I can't come to rehearsal tomorrow I've got to go and count owls with my uncle in the animal refuge.

Not every student will display humor or lyricism or even imagination, but this isn't a talent search. The fundamental goal is to help free the students' imagination before it disappears or becomes programmed and in doing so, to help them acquire the tools to express themselves.

Aim: To write in someone else's voice.

Exercise 7.2: Ask your students to go off and write, not as themselves but as a character, a reason why he or she didn't make it to rehearsal. Again, the piece should be no longer than three minutes and no shorter than two lines. When the students return this time, have them pass their writing around. Each student should read another's piece.

Example: (Old lady) I'm sorry I can't come to rehearsal tomorrow, I've got arthritis and bunions and I can't walk.

Aim: To create character.

Exercise 7.3: Ask each of your students to go off and write a monologue about how beautiful he or she is. Same time allotments. When the students return, ask each one to read his or her monologue and find a fitting walk while he or she is reading it.

Example: I am so hot that the fire alarm goes off every time I walk by it. I got the eyes of a tiger, better hair than Cher, and oh, my body causes the girls to go down on their knees and pray. (This boy has the strut of a body builder. He turns and shows his beauty as if he is a Calvin Klein model.)

Aim: Incorporating another voice into your monologue.

Exercise 7.4: Write a monologue about your best friend, why you like her, and what you do together. Put a line in expressing how she talks.

Example: My best friend is Sue. She is almost six feet tall and has sad eyes and short brown hair. She's very dreamy and sometimes she stops talking and just stares as if she's looking out on the ocean. I ask her what she's thinking about and she always says something like, "I'm wondering what it would be like to be right now sitting on a mat in a small town in Japan drawing flowers with those wooden brushes. I wish I could live two lives." Sue is crazy like that and I love her.

Aim: Remembering another voice.

Exercise 7.5: Teach us a subject in the voice of your least favorite teacher.

Example: Mrs. Alexander yells at our history class. "You *will* sit down," she says, "and you *will* take out your textbooks, and if you *could* act like civilized people we *will* begin our discussion on Roosevelt and World War II."

Aim: Recalling a live moment.

Exercise 7.6: Write about a time when you did something really crazy—*good* crazy.

Example: Sandy's mom collects music boxes and one day when we were alone in her house, we turned on all the music boxes at the same time—I mean, like a hundred of them. It sounded like we were in a crazy circus.

Aim: To hear two voices.

Exercise 7.7: Write a scene for you and a friend. You're talking about something you really agree on. Let's hear you agreeing with each other.

Example:
SARAH: Tom is so cute.
JEAN: He is really cute.
SARAH: I like his hair.
JEAN: I like his hair too.

Adjustment:

Liz says, "Ladies, is that how you really talk? Like pod people? Can't I know more? What's so great about his hair anyway?"

Rewrite:

SARAH: *Oh oh oh*, there's Tom!

JEAN: He is *cute*.

SARAH: I think he's got a sweet face like Leonardo DiC*a*prio.

JEAN: Yeah, except his hair is this beautiful almost blond color.

SARAH: Sun-bleached.

JEAN: And it's wavy.

SARAH: Like a surfer.

JEAN: Yeah, I know, and those T-shirts he wears with those stupid
   sayings on them, like "Dracula Sucks."

Aim: To record conflict.

Exercise 7.8: Write a description of a fight—you and someone else really disagreeing over something. Or write about a fight you've heard about.

Example:

SAM: You're ugly.

JAY: You're stupid.

SAM: Your face is stupid.

JAY: You have a weird nose.

Adjustment:

Liz: "That's great, and I'm sure people talk like that. But you're just insulting each other, you're not fighting *over* anything."

Rewrite:

SAM: You're so slow, you make a turtle look like NASCAR.

JAY: I can beat you in a second. My feet are wind.

SAM: I am a jet plane in sneakers.

JAY: You can't beat me.

SAM: You can't beat *me*.

JAY: I am definitely faster than you.

SAM: You're crazy. I'm a winner.

JAY: I'm the winner.

Aim: To work on building.

Exercise 7.9: Create a fight over something small that gets bigger and ends up going into a whole history of problems. Have the writer read the piece out loud with a partner.

Example:

LISA: That dollar is mine.

ANN: What? It's *mine*.

LISA: I know it dropped right out of my bag.

ANN: I left it here.

LISA: You're lying.

ANN: You always lie.

LISA: Me? You lie all the time.

ANN: Yeah? About what?

LISA: You said you got an A in history, but you didn't, you got a
    C minus.

ANN: What, are you looking in my books?

LISA: No, I saw when she gave it back.

ANN: You are such a nosy bitch.

LISA: You gonna curse at me now?

ANN: What—you don't have a dirty mouth? What're you, my mother?

LISA: Your mother? Who'd want to be your mother?

ANN: Well, she's better than yours.

LISA: You want to get into mothers?

(and so on)

Remind your students that it's important to take into account that his or her writing is to be performed out loud. Therefore, it has to be dramatic and have a voice as well as the rhythms of the character who is speaking.

PERSONAL AND TOPICAL WRITING ASSIGNMENTS

1. Write a monologue about a fight you had or heard within your family and how it affected you. Remember: You can tell a real story or make one up—but it has to be believable.

2. Issue-oriented: Write a description of someone you've seen who was drunk or high. What did he or she look like? Act like? What did he say or how did he talk?

3. Write a short scene between a parent and a child in which the parent is furious—justly or unjustly—at the child.

4. Write a scene in which a bad kid or adult pressures you into sex, drugs, crime, or violence.

5. Write a story about losing a person or a pet. Describe the person or pet and how it feels to have suffered this loss.

6. Give some advice to a friend who is down and out on how he or she can pull himself or herself together.

7. Write a piece in which you comfort someone; remember to be specific about what his or her grief is about.

8. Write a monologue telling off a teacher, parent, or friend.

9. Write an apology.

10. Write about a time when you were really scared for the world — or if not the world, then for your family or friends.

11. Write a piece about feeling really down (and why), feeling like an outsider and rejected, not cool, excluded.

12. Write a piece about what you would fix in your life if you had the power and the choice.

13. Write a story about someone who got in trouble.

14. Write a story about humiliation — yours or someone else's.

15. Write about something of which you're really proud.

16. Write a story about behavior or an action that was really ridiculous.

17. Write a scene in which one person is threatening the other.

18. Write a scene in which one person is flirting with another.

19. Write a scene in which one person is trying to persuade the other to have sex.

20. Write a monologue from the point of view of someone:
    a. who feels violent
    b. who is high
    c. who has run away
    d. who is hurting
    e. who has AIDS

21. Write a scene about kids treating each other badly or well.

22. Write a monologue or scene about someone who is addicted to surfing the Internet.

23. Write a story or monologue about the meeting of a student and another character through the Internet. Make it:

   a. funny
   b. strange
   c. loving
   d. dangerous

24. Write a monologue or scene about a student who's feeling pressured to be number one.

25. Write about a time you were treated differently because of:

   a. race
   b. religion
   c. looks
   d. age
   e. sexuality
   f. gender

26. Write about a time you treated someone differently because of his or her:

   a. race
   b. religion
   c. looks
   d. age
   e. sexuality

27. Write about a violent event that affected you:

   a. in your neighborhood
   b. in your school
   c. in your house
   d. in the world

28. Write a scene in which you come out to your parents or friends. (The reaction doesn't always have to be horrible.)

29. Write a monologue in which you question whether you're gay or not.

30. Write about a time when a teacher picked on you unfairly. Let's hear the voice of the teacher in the story.

31. Write about an adult who surprised you by acting in an unexpected way. What did he or she say or do?

32. Write about a song that moves you deeply. Why does it move you? Describe the singer.

USING THE IMAGINATION

Here are writing exercises for students who want to create a fairy tale, legend, myth, or science fiction:

1. Write a monologue from the point of view of an alien seeing Earth for the first time.

2. Write a scene between an alien and a human who are meeting for the first time.

3. Write a monologue about what it's like to be half horse and half human.

4. Write about your extra-special strengths and powers, focusing on:
    a. whom you rescued or are going to rescue
    b. a great deed you did or are going to do

5. Write a scene in which you tell a friend what it was like to live with the trolls or fight against an intergalactic army.

6. Call your troops into battle; make sure they're ready for what's ahead.

7. Write a story about what it's like to be in love with an alien, and have no one believe you.

8. Write a monologue from the point of view of a witch who's making a plan to create a stew out of children.

9. Talk about a time when you were kidnapped:

   a. by aliens

   b. by an evil enemy from the forest

10. Describe your brilliant new invention.

11. Talk about time travel. What decades did you travel to and what did you see on your visits?

12. Describe who lives in your closet. What does he or she or it say?

13. Write about an angel, god, or demon who has visited you lately. What did he or she want?

14. You have been crowned king or queen or president of a whole country.

    a. What are some of your laws?

    b. Where do you live?

    c. How will you treat your people?

15. Describe an intergalactic/interplanetary rock concert.

    a. What does the music sound like?

    b. What do the bands look like?

16. Write, from an alien's point of view, your opinion about what is right or wrong with America.

17. Write a scene between two robots (or computers).

18. Write a love scene between a robot (or computer) and a human.

ADAPTING STUDENTS' WORK

If you find that some or all of your students' writing is not specific or clear enough to use in a final work, you or other writers may want to edit those students' spontaneous words to put them into a form that will work onstage. Many professional theater ensembles do weeks of improvisation and discussion while a writer watches and listens. Later, this spontaneity is transformed into a written theater piece.

Here are some examples of my adaptations of young actors' exact words.

In the following scene, I made very few changes. I rearranged sentences and played with the length but kept the content intact. I tried hard not to lose the tone and rhythm of each voice.

A.J.

I was walking down Allentown Avenue one night.
And I saw this man.
And I just wanted to walk by him.
As I was walking by him, he walked up to me.
He said: "Do you have any money?"
And I said: "No."
Then he pulled out this huge knife.
And I looked at it and pushed him and he fell.
So I started to run.
I didn't know if he was going to get up and chase me again.
There was no one there to save me.

ROBY

I was coming home from school one night,
And I came the way I usually do along this long block that was
    badly lit,
And there was this man standing by the school park.
And he looked really freaky,
And I wanted to get by him so I could go about my business.
And as I walked by him all he said was: "Sinner."
And I looked at him as if to say,

Why are you bothering me. I haven't done anything to you.
But he just kept saying: "Sinner."
And "It started with the blood,
And every month you bleed, you sin."

JACKIE

I remember the night of my tenth birthday.
We were driving in my mom's car.
She was drunk and I had to drive the car for her,
And I couldn't find the way home.
So this cop car pulled up and said for us
To get in the back seat,
And I told 'em her name.
I felt really awful 'cause the next morning she was supposed to
    hold a big birthday party for me.
And the next morning she really showed up out of the jailhouse.
And she'd fixed herself all up.

—from *Runaways*

Here is an example of how I transformed the spontaneous ideas
of my students into words:

JOYCE: Let's talk about mothers.

ANNIE: I don't like this topic. It's boring. We have to be with our
    mothers all the time. Why talk about them now?

JOYCE: I'm my mother's mother. She says so all the time. If it wasn't
    for me, she says I wouldn't have been born. I told her to have me.

NESSA: What?

JOYCE: She's psychic, she heard me before she made me.

SARAH: Not another drugged girl made from the sixties.

JOYCE: My mother never takes drugs. She's vegan and does prana yana twice a day.

ANNIE: That's drugs to me. Same space and generation.

NESSA: I don't have any idea as to what my mom does. She works for some healing organization, but I don't know what she heals or does.

SARAH: My mother's main purpose in life is to tell me to brush my hair. I can see her after not seeing her for two months and she'd say hello darling, brush that hair out of your eyes. "Oh! You cut yourself. Don't get your hair bloody." Just kidding.

GINA: But let's go back a bit. What do Jewish healers do?

NESSA: I'm telling you, I've been trying to figure that one out for years.

CHLOE: Touch is important to the healing process. You know those AIDS babies that die because no one touches them?

ANNIE: They die because they have AIDS.

CHLOE: You know what I mean. Music can heal. I can't go to sleep without music.

ANNIE: Animals help me heal. I just put my arms around one of my dogs.

MICKEY: My mom's like my friend. She's all into—how do I feel about this and how do I feel about that. It freaks her out if I tell her I'm not feeling anything in particular. Then she pushes harder because she thinks I'm covering up some really deep feeling.

NESSA: My mother's a Buddhist too.

(Hits a gong.)

ANNIE: They say the rich have the luxury to practice spirituality. The poor are too busy surviving reality.

CHLOE: But my mom's very generous. She does charity events, raises money for this, for that, for the homeless, for the aged, for the survivors of war, for the people with pebbles in their shoes.

MICKEY: No time for you, huh?

CHLOE: Oh no. Lots of time for me. Too much time for me. My mother talks to me, not at me.

AMANDA: She's always checking her nails. She herself has bright red fingernails and has to leave the house with perfect heels. I practice your basic Category A rebellion. But I don't work on it. I truly don't like red fingernails and I'm not in the least charitable.

JOYCE: My mother's one of my best friends. It's all about respect like the *Gilmore Girls*.

—from *Jewish Girlz*

You can also make an original piece with your students that does not involve *their* writing. Ask them to research and bring in poems, favorite stories, newspaper articles, advertisements, plus any of the ensemble's original writing that strikes you as performable. When I was guest director at Harvard in 2000 (and later at NYU), the students and I made a piece for the millennium consisting of selected writings from anthologies. We used lines only from unknown writers in their teens and twenties—and only material that reflected what life was like for young people in the late twentieth century. You can use classic writing as well, as long as your students help choose and perform the material. Imagine your theme and find writing that fits—from sources as varied as Emily Dickinson and Snoop Dogg.

I want my students to experience a genuine sense of ownership of the texts that make up their show. This not only boosts individual self-esteem, but also makes for more impassioned acting and thus better performances. If the final show is a well-made machine of emotion and story, the students will perform it with commitment and pride. I'm adamant in feeling that what's best for students is, in the final analysis, very good theater. This is why my high school ensembles can perform in front of their peers in public schools, community centers, and group homes without being heckled or shouted down. If there are weak moments, young audiences will turn the auditorium into a rock club and, believe me, the show is over. I learned this in other countries as well. If you don't have a good show, a whole community will turn its back, laugh, and converse about day-to-day subjects. You'll end up doing the show for a stampede.

For instance, once on the African tour I described in the Introduction, the actors performed in a lively town in Nigeria. They were tired and arguing a bit among themselves. The improv that they came up with reflected their fatigue. The children in the audience started getting restless and buzzing like hives of bees, then the parents took the opportunity to catch up on business and gossip. Soon the center of town resembled a noisy market. Finally, a light that we were using to light the area broke, which became the event to see. Obviously, the audience was much more interesting than the company, with the result that the actors had to leave the stage. The lesson we learned was that a theater group must be close-knit, vibrant in their timing, and as conscious of one another's words as basketball players are of the ball being dribbled toward the opposite basket.

EIGHT

SPACE

THEATER IS special because it is live. Actors sing, act, and move around in a space, so the space in which you make theater is as important as any other element in the mix.

The space where you perform is a home for your created work. Usually the first step in composing that space comes when a set designer looks with a visual artist's eye at the possibilities of the stage. The designer thinks about the colors and shapes that will be behind and beside, above and below, the action. But bear in mind that a set can be *anything*. A drama may require a naturalistic living room and kitchen. If a character is a writer, there might be a large bookshelf. If she is a cook, the focus might be on an array of pots and pans. A set can represent a forest. Diverse materials are bunched together to make the trees or paths. Or a set can consist of two blocks, displaying a neutral stage in which a story can change in the imagination. There are several types of conventional theaters: proscenium, thrust, three-quarters, in the round. The design of the stage defines the relationship of the actors to the audience, how they will see, how immediate the action is, and even the point of view of the play.

These choices are the job of the designer, but it is important for

the student to understand and appreciate space. These days everything from a black box to a high school bathroom can be labeled a
setting for theater. Whatever the location, the student has to be aware
of how he or she as a performer can best use the space. I think it's useful for students to get used to working without frills—to make what
Antonin Artaud called "poor theater," which means that you do your
play in an environment in which nothing but the actors and the audience is essential. If the performance can enliven the stage without
set or costumes, it is a show that is working on human spirit and drive
alone. Real theater is not dependent on expensive special effects but
on the vibrancy of the live performance.

When actors don't use their natural voices in a production and
instead depend on complex sound systems, the space is redefined by
the sound design. When a multilayered set fills the stage, the production is influenced by the power of the set. Audiences will experience
a sense of wonder at the spectacle. But the theater I am talking about
uses nothing to distract the audience from basic human passion and
the power of the actors' spirits. A performance of such a play should
be a unique adventure, shared by the audience and the actors.

When I was nineteen, I worked with Andrei Serban on a version
of *Medea*. The production was in a small basement; benches were
placed against the walls for the audience. I think we could sit forty to
fifty people a night. Andrei wanted the fury and ritual of the Greek
tragedy to be close and resonant. Later on, he created a version of *The
Trojan Women* in which, once again, the audience was part of the ritual, like worshippers in a church or synagogue. Since the piece was
about a whole city, the audience was led around a vast warehouse
building by actors carrying torches. They were stopped at specific
wooden platforms where the prophecies of violence against and en-
slavement of the surviving women of Troy took place. A large wooden
cage holding the doomed Astianax was carried into the audience—
and another cage holding a cursing Helen of Troy was rolled back

and forth. Andrei had Andromache kill herself by diving off a ledge seemingly into the crowd. (A 1970s version of the mosh pit was there instead, with actors to catch her.) Serban's use of space was the beginning of a trend, as many have now followed his lead. The question is often asked in theater, How can you involve the audience in a visual way? Now, in shows like *De La Guarda*, actors fly over the audience, even pour water over them. In Blue Man Group performances, blue actors sometimes carry audience members into hidden rooms.

I'll never forget the feeling of performing in the Sahara Desert, or in the vibrant, noisy North African villages, balancing on the ruins of the temple of Venus in Baalbek, Lebanon, or watching a cast of singers crowd the center archways in Jerusalem's Temple of David. Actors use their voices differently in every space, they feel their bodies' energy rise and fall according to different heights and distances. They learn to live in a space so that they can "fill it"—which means using its every corner, crevice, and shadow.

Spaces don't have to be as exotic as the ones I've mentioned, but a vision has to be there for the entire area, from the largest expanse of land to the tiniest corner. When I first started out, one of my friends was a puppeteer, Robbie Anton, who has tragically been lost to AIDS, but who during his life made the most extraordinary puppets the size of a finger. He started out entertaining an audience of two at a time, on a stage that consisted of a small wooden box, a candle, and his body. He floated his puppets, lit by the candle, in front of the black velvet cover of his upper body, making the puppets come to life. Those of us who saw the early shows were alone with Robbie, the puppets, and one other audience member—a truly mysterious and wonderful experience. Individuals would wait months to get on his private list, and in time his work became immensely popular. He was invited to festivals all over the world. He then expanded his theater to the size of a coffee table for an audience of twelve.

How does a student learn about the space to be inhabited? For a full understanding you would have to go to architecture school, practice landscaping, or learn set or movie design. The exercises that follow, however, have been developed to help the students explore their space with their senses and imagination. As directors and actors become more committed to a total theater, they know that the specific sites are an intrinsic part of the whole. Every theatrical space, whether conventional or not, is a new challenge.

Vocal Exploration of Space

Aim: To experience one's own size and volume.

Exercise 8.1: The students should walk, run, sit, climb, shout, and whisper within the chosen space to feel it freely and take in its size and acoustics.

Aim: To experience the group's dynamics in different distances.

Exercise 8.2: Stand together in a circle. All the students should begin quickly saying the phrase "Three blind mice, three blind mice." Say it over and over as very slowly you widen the circle until the students are spread as far apart as possible, then start to come together again.

1. As the circle spreads apart, your voices should become louder and louder. As the circle moves in, the voices become softer and softer.
2. As the circle spreads apart, the voices become softer and softer. As the circle comes together, the voices become louder and louder.

Concentrate on the gradual up-and-down of the dynamics. Listen to how the sound of the group changes as you move from close to far, from a small area of space to a much bigger landscape.

Aim: To test your voice in the room.

Exercise 8.3: Spread out in the space. Have each student make an individual long, calling sound—a sustained tone. Do it straight ahead, to the sky, and to the ground. Listen to how the sound differs in each direction.

Exercise 8.4: Make a sound and try to fill the whole space with it, but direct it toward the person farthest away. Are you making a round sound? A sharp sound? Consonants? Vowels?

1. Go back and forth in the space, trying to make the exact same sound.
2. Go back and forth using different sounds, but with the same intention of calling back and forth.
3. Go back and forth and change your sounds to match the basic form of the first two sounds, but improvise with pitch and length and texture of sounds. Stress consonants, stress vowels, play with rhythm, then play with different accents on chosen syllables. Listen to which sounds carry and which don't. Listen to which sounds reach the other people and which sounds don't.

Aim: To hear and respond to distant sounds.

Exercise 8.5: Now exchange calls with two or three other students far away. Can you sustain the clarity or intensity of each sound?

Exercise 8.6: Try calling the same sounds in different physical positions.

1. Standing straight
2. Leaning forward
3. Leaning backward

4. Sitting

5. Kneeling

How does the shape of your body change the sound?

Exercise 8.7: Repeat these exercises, but now move through the space toward one another, as if in a relay race.

1. Walk past one another.

2. Circle one another.

3. Pass close to one another.

4. Walk backward.

5. Hop or jog.

6. Crawl.

7. Slither on your belly.

Keep listening to how the sounds change in the space. Keep your attention on how the sounds relate to the space and to one another's sounds.

Aim: To learn to hear the distant acoustics in the space.

Exercise 8.8: Spread out through the space, going as far as possible. One student should make a long sustained calling sound toward another, taking care to direct the sound explicitly toward that person. The student who receives the call then responds.

Visual Exploration of Space

Aim: To explore the space visually—to expand your visual vocabulary.

Exercise 8.9:

1. Have each student find a section of the space that inspires a particular body position or self-made picture. The students then stay still. Students might:

   a. Crouch in a corner.
   b. Lie on a couch.
   c. Hide behind a couch.
   d. Stand on a desk.
   e. Curl up under a desk.
   f. Fill a doorway.
   g. Lie in the middle of the floor.
   h. Stand flat against a wall.

2. Visualize how you look in the whole space.

   a. As a picture
   b. As a silent scene

3. Does the shape of your body against the whole space evoke an emotional situation?

   a. Hiding
   b. Showing off
   c. Possessing something
   d. Being glamorous
   e. Being a monster
   f. Being a child
   g. Becoming an inanimate object

Exercise 8.10: Do this same exercise, using two or three bodies in the same section of the space.

1. Two students in a corner: What does the image evoke?

2. Two students sitting at one desk: What emotions are suggested by their proximity?

3. Two students sitting under a desk: How does this express "hiding"?

4. Three students flat against the wall: What separate interpretations can there be of this image?

Improvise different pictures (or tableaux) using as many bodies as you wish, but concentrate on how the pictures relate to the whole space. Use placing as part of the picture so that if bodies took the same positions in another setting, the final picture would be different.

Exercise 8.11: Repeat these visual exercises and add sound. Pay attention to how the space and physical positions influence the voices. Start to look at the bodies in their pictures as the beginning of a story. What is the story?

INDOOR AND OUTDOOR USE OF SPACE

I've written of my collaborator Andrei Serban, the first director I worked with who used space as an essential part of drama. As I've written, I met him when he was visiting the La MaMa Theatre after he had spent a year in Paris working with Peter Brook. He had more than just a painter's eye: he saw theater as a living event in which it was as important for the audience to experience a scene physically as it was to watch or listen to it. I worked with Andrei for seven years at La MaMa and composed music for nine different shows that he created. We worked both indoors and outdoors, and because of him, my whole concept of what a "stage" might be was transformed.

As I've said, our first production, *Medea*, took place in a basement. The nurse and chorus led the audience through a small dark corridor toward the "stage," which was a tiny room. The nurse and chorus whispered urgently in the corridor of Medea's plight, and you could hear her screaming curses from the basement room. Serban used the terror of a fun house with the deeper sense of foreboding that comes with Greek tragedy. Once inside, the audience couldn't leave without stepping right through the action. The space made you a prisoner. The chorus sat on boxes directly next to the audience members; the audience sat on benches on opposite sides of the room, facing one another as they would at a football game. Medea and Jason faced each other across a tiny platform. The space was almost completely dark, and the actors held candles. The audience and actors were so close to one another that the actual vibrations of the actors' voices could be physically felt—whispers gave chills—and Medea's screams permeated the atmosphere in such a violent manner that you felt as if you were in a madhouse. Eventually the chorus became a group of ritualistic worshippers transformed by Medea's evil, as they chanted and danced a polyrhythmic chorus, holding a pot of fire and passing it wildly from one initiate to the next. The proximity of the wildly dancing actors to the audience was part of what made the ritual so diabolical—and so effective.

As in most great tragedies, the crucial action—in this case, the killing of Medea's children—took place offstage. But the chorus's dance of death gave the audience a direct involvement with the hedonistic quality of the murders. Finally, the dead children were lowered from a trapdoor in the ceiling onto the shoulders of the broken father, Jason. You felt as if something dark and otherworldly were taking place above your head. Then Medea herself hung upside down from the same trapdoor like a monstrous bat, goading Jason and letting the audience know that she had done what she had to do and was now at peace. At the end, the audience was alone in the tiny dark space, staring at one another. Large clay masks lit by flickering candles sat where the chorus had been. Never once had an audience member been touched or violated, but because of the way Andrei used the space, they were thrown viscerally into the drama.

Later on Andrei Serban restaged *Medea* many times, in locations all over the world. I watched as he worked within each space to create the same immediacy for the audience. He didn't try to replicate the La MaMa basement—he studied each theater or ancient ruin and let the mystery of each locale influence the way *Medea* would be staged. In 1973 this was a revolutionary concept. Today, the kind of theater that is influenced by a space is called "site specific," and certain theater makers find whole buildings, parks, or waterfronts to suit their vision.

Andrei and Ellen Stewart of La MaMa designed the large warehouse facility I spoke of earlier. It was called the La MaMa Annex. As the audience moved from place to place to witness fragments from the doomed lives of the survivors in Andrei's staging of *The Trojan Women*, they themselves experienced what it was like to be in the role of a prisoner. When soldiers yelled orders and, holding torches, forced the women to move from platform to platform, the audience was startled by the sound of sticks pounded on the ground. The cries of the women and the shouting of the soldiers took place at seemingly random moments and in places right where the audience stood. *The Trojan Women* was ahead of its time, and I think you'll see that a description of this work is an appropriate prelude to my thoughts about staging.

Exploration of Space Using Movement

Aim: To visualize scenes in various settings.

Exercise 8.12: One student leads the group through the space as a tour guide. He or she "describes" the imagined walls and furniture— the most basic elements in the room—however he or she chooses.

1. Make a story around the space and objects.

Example: This desk is where John Timmons fired Johnson Moon and Moon came back and threw glue over all the office workers and this paper.

2. Give the space itself a made-up history.

Example: As we walk along this wall, we can make out the faint handprints of the Indian who lived at this corner before us.

3. Objectively describe exactly what is there.

Example: Here's the place where we usually "circle up," and this is one of the bathrooms, but the girls like the one downstairs.

Two or three other students should conduct the same "tour" with their own variations. This way you can see how objects, shapes, and space affect each student's imagination differently.

Aim: To take in an area with the senses and the imagination.

Exercise **8.13:** The group casually walks around the space together until a chosen leader yells out, "Pose!" Each student takes a frozen position right where she or he is in the space, using the location to help shape the pose.

I particularly like to take my NYU classes on the streets of downtown New York to see how they'll utilize what's around them. Doing the exercise this way can provide a spontaneous improvisational show for the shoppers and citizens who happen to be in the neighborhood.

Example: We're walking on the sidewalk by the front of an apartment building. I yell out, "Freeze!"

Person 1 freezes in the revolving door of the apartment building as if caught in a fish tank.

Person 2 stands flat against a wall as if posing for a Calvin Klein ad.

Person 3 stands on the curb as if hailing a taxi.

Person 4 leans against a lamppost like a 1940s gangster.

Person 5 freezes on the corner begging for change.

We walk farther and go through Washington Square Park. At a certain point I say "Freeze."

Person 1 freezes on a park bench, lying down as if asleep.

Person 2 freezes behind a tree as if playing hide and seek.

Person 3 freezes outside the dog park on all fours.

Person 4 freezes as if playing a saxophone for tips.

Person 5 jumps into the fountain, freezes in the water, and
cracks everybody up.

Aim: Staging the beginning of a scene.

Exercise 8.14: Now we add language and movement to the exercise. Once again we're inside. We walk around the rehearsal space, and I say, "Stop." The students take positions and do simple repetitive movements.

Example:

John sits at a table in the space miming eating soup.

Sam stands looking over John's shoulder.

Max is leaning against a wall at the far side of the room.

Jane finds a broom and starts to sweep.

Alex is going in and out of the door, continually in and out.

At this point the students don't relate to each other; they take inspiration from their positions and objects. Then they find a sentence to repeat over and over.

JOHN: This is great soup, it's really great—creamed crabapple soup.

SAM: What are you eating? It looks terrible—why are you eating that?

MAX: I DON'T WANT TO STAY HERE. I'LL BE GOOD—I PROMISE.

JANE: I always get the chores. No one else does them, so I'm stuck with the chores.

ALEX: Okay, goodbye. Oops, I forgot something. Okay, really goodbye—oops, I forgot something.

If the students do this exercise outdoors, they should use a park or playground where they can spread out. If they can't find a park or playground, they can use a quiet street and work from a far corner to a near one.

Exercise 8.15: The students take positions in a space, indoors or outdoors. This time, they watch and listen to one another carefully and improvise a scene together. Since they are incorporating the space, their bodies, and one another's words, the text will often come out sounding goofy. It's a victory if you can just keep the text coherent.

Example: Outside—in a playground.

John runs around the basketball hoop, shooting imaginary baskets.

Sam stands in a corner, isolated.

Max crouches in the middle of the space, playing with an imaginary toy.

Jane is with Max; they play together.

Alex looks out through the surrounding fence.

JOHN: I'm gonna get this shot. Watch me, I'm gonna get this, I am the basketball God. (*to Sam*) Wanna play?

SAM: I can't. You know I don't know how.

MAX and JANE: Shut up, we don't care about your stupid game. Ken and Barbie are sleeping.

ALEX: (*to John*) You always brag. I'm waiting for Joe. He'll beat your sorry butt.

JOHN: Oh yeah? Let him try. I'm the basketball God.

ALEX: You have such a big head.

JOHN: (*to Sam*) What's wrong with you? I'll teach you.

SAM: You're gonna pull some trick. You're a bully.

JOHN: Come here, I'll show you how a champion plays.

MAX and JANE: (*to John and Sam*) Shut up, our dolls are having a very important conversation. (*They talk in doll voices*)

JOHN: I'm gonna bounce my basketball right on their heads.

MAX: You're just a bully.

SAM: I can't learn from you—you're too mean.

JOHN: Stop whining. I'm not mean. I just get the job done.

ALEX: Yeah, here comes Joe—he's gonna beat your butt.

JOHN: (*mockingly*) Oh, I'm scared. He can't beat me, I am the basketball God.

JANE: (*to John*) You always ruin everything with your big loud mouth.

JOHN: (*to Sam*) Come on, I'll teach ya.

MAX: He'll teach you and then punch you.

   (and so on)

As I said, the content of the improvisations will be silly and only *just* make sense. The idea is to use the characters, space, position, movement, and a modest plot in an unfamiliar locale.

Aim: To understand differences in staging.

Exercise 8.16: In a chosen space, a student recites or improvises a monologue with the specific direction to pay attention and fully use the space he or she occupies (chairs, tables, walls, props). Then he or she goes to a completely different space and does the same monologue, adapting to the new space. The teacher and students observe how the feeling of the text itself changes:

1. Inside a small space
2. In a large space
3. Outside
4. In different poses in relation to different objects

NINE

TIME

LIFE TAKES PLACE in its own time. Since theater is a heightened reflection of life, the sense of time in theater is often also heightened, subject to a different reality. Without real sensitivity to dynamics— that is, long and short, fast and slow—a student can't find all the keys that can make a show truly dramatic. Feeling the rightness of tempo becomes an instinct, but I have found that there are ways, from the beginning of the process, to develop the student's sensitivity to pace and tempo.

The following are guidelines to help develop an internal sense of time.

1. Every single exercise should take place in a given period of time. No exercises should be open-ended.

2. Individual work should be kept to a pace at which the student succeeds in keeping intention and concentration for as much of his or her presentation as possible. This includes simple movements in the circle to full-out scene work.

3. Keep improvs and demonstrations on the short side. There's

nothing that sucks out energy more than going on and on in a repetitive, static improv or presentation of work.

4. Instill the sense of time in all students by giving them exact times for everything. Examples:

  a. You have three minutes to create a dance step.

  b. You have five minutes to go and create an improv on (subject).

  c. Bring in a character but allow him or her to talk for only one minute.

  d. Create a three-minute circus in which everything goes wrong. You have twenty minutes.

  e. You have a half hour to write a monologue on (subject). The monologue can't be longer than a page and a half.

I try to create an atmosphere in which one minute is an acceptable amount of time and three minutes is a luxury. I don't sit with a stopwatch, but these time rules make every second valuable and therefore help the student begin to understand how time is used on stage.

As students are spread out while creating their assignments, I shout out the time as it passes.

"You have two minutes to go!"

"You have twenty seconds!"

I insist that when the time is up, the time *is* up. When students work at home, they can take as long as they want, but in rehearsal, time is a constant presence. I don't let students linger, even if they say, "Oh, give us two more minutes, please, just *two* more minutes." This teaches students how much they can accomplish in a short period of time, makes time exceedingly valuable, and presents the notion that being an artist requires as much efficiency as imagination.

I believe that respect for time makes the work less stressful for the student, because they have to "get it done," not argue or ruminate. I discourage long discussions while preparing improvs and hope they learn to communicate by doing, showing, demonstrating, and practicing with one another. I don't tolerate little secret dictators or bullies. This is a time during which I watch carefully to see how each student is doing. If the students don't finish what they're supposed to within my time span, I emphasize that it's not important. I ask them to show me what they've got. If we all like the idea, they can go off and work on it later. I am less strict about the product itself. The exercises aren't contests to see who can do best in the shortest amount of time. Therefore, if a group creates an interesting sequence but is unable to complete it, there's no reason to punish them. Their sense of time will be challenged and they will work faster the next time—and you can also show the students that even an unfinished fragment can be the seed of an exciting theatrical piece.

By the end of the rehearsal process, students will understand that ten minutes is a vast, luxurious, and often dangerous amount of time in which a relationship can build and end or a bit of history can be presented or, in some cases, an entire play can take place.

General Time Exercises

Aim: To give students a sense of dynamics.

Exercise 9.1: In the circle, each student presents a movement. He or she should teach it to the others and have them do it as fast as they can, then as slowly as they can. Then they should go back to the original tempo.

Exercise 9.2: Each student makes a phrase of abstract vocal sounds. He or she teaches it to the group, then does it as fast as possible and as slowly as possible. Then they should go back to the original tempo.

Exercise 9.3: Each student should make up a dance step, show it, and teach it to the group. This time, have the group do it gradually faster, then gradually slower.

Exercise 9.4: Each student should present a sentence in English. The group should learn the sentence and then repeat it, listening carefully to one another and speeding up a little every repetition, until they are going as fast as possible without being sloppy.

Exercise 9.5: Divide a sentence up around the circle, giving each student a word.

Go around the circle and find a rhythm. It should feel like a single voice is saying the sentence. See if you can gradually speed up the speaking of the sentence without losing the basic clarity and pace.

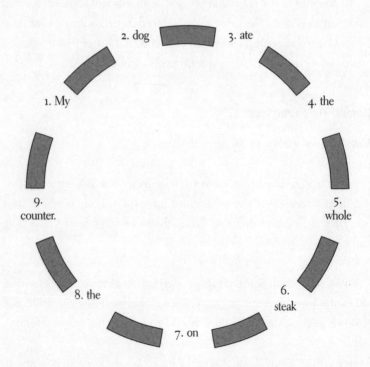

2. dog   3. ate

1. My   4. the

9.   5.
counter.   whole

8. the   6.
                         steak

          7. on

Aim: To develop an internal sense of time.

Exercise 9.6: Sit in a circle. Have one student talk about any topic in a normal casual tone. For example: "I read a new book today about this guy who went into Bosnia with a circus troop delivering food to the poor . . ." The student keeps talking. The other students are told to call out when they think ten seconds have passed, then twenty seconds. Check their guesses against a stop watch.

Aim: To learn how to create a "build" within a given amount of time.

Exercise 9.7: Do what I call "the stupid stress dance." I encourage the students to make—and then do—a dance that gets crazier and crazier within the space of two minutes; then one minute; then thirty seconds.

Exercise 9.8: Have the students walk around the room at a regular pace, then have one student or the teacher call out commands, which the group should obey:

1. Faster
2. Slower
3. Very very slow
4. Even slower
5. Very very fast
6. The fastest ever
7. Even faster
8. You have never been so slow in your life
   (and so on)

Exercise 9.9: Ask a student to come forward and "bore us." How is time involved in the measuring of what presentation is alive and what is dead?

Exercise 9.10: Have several students "bore you." Examine the differences in each student's purposeful misuse of time. Encourage pauses, repetitions, slowness, speed that is not understandable, monotone, and shrieking.

Aim: To experience passage of time in the voice.

Exercise 9.11: Ask each student to take a sustained tone and build it gradually in pitch and volume so he can feel every step along the way. When is the building too fast? Too slow?

Aim: To see how the use of time affects scenes.

Exercise 9.12: Create a short scene (or take an existing one) and try it at different tempos. Then do the same scene at a "natural tempo." Compare the dramatic effect to the other dynamics—the other tempos. Finally, do the scene and build it in a natural way so that the timing feels right.

TO OFFER an example of a build, I like to play my students a recording of Otis Redding singing "Try a Little Tenderness." This song starts with rhythm at a slow bluesy pace and, several minutes later, it organically builds to a riotous funky beat that feels as though it has reached the top of its energy. (If you prefer, you can choose a movement from a symphonic work.)

Aim: To feel the effect of timing on entrances and exits.

Exercise 9.13: A student divides the entire group into four smaller groups. This "conductor" gives each group a *separate repeated sound* or *phrase* (either with or without a specific beat). The conductor conducts the groups, creating a "soundscape" or a "story made of sound" (a chorus of sounds that reflects an emotion or place or story). The voices can go in and out one or two at a time or all together. By bringing groups in and out, the conductor creates and tells a story.

Example: A zoo at feeding time. Distribution of sounds:

1	2	3	4
lions	peacocks	elephants	seals
roar	squawk	honk	howl

A possible sequence as created by the conductor:

1. The seals howl for food.
2. The peacocks answer.
3. The elephants honk.
4. The lions roar.
5. The animals get louder and angrier as they get more hungry.
6. The sound reaches a deafening peak.
7. One by one the animals get fed. They quiet down.
8. The peacocks are the last to be fed. They squawk like crazy.
9. Peacocks get fed.
10. The whole zoo is quiet and mellow.

Example: A soundscape at an auction. Distribution of sounds:

1	2	3	4
snobby lady	foreign man	old woman	auctioneer
high voice	voice with accent	old voice	auctioneer's voice

A possible dialogue:

AUCTIONEER: What do I hear for this lovely iron stove?

FOREIGNER: Seventy thousand rupees.

SNOBBY LADY: I bid a thousand dollars, dear.

OLD LADY: It's an ugly piece of junk. Ha.

A possible sequence as created by the conductor:

1. The auctioneer asks for bids.
2. The foreigner starts.
3. The old lady mocks him and laughs.
4. The foreigner bids again — angrily.
5. The snobby lady bids.
6. The old lady mocks her and laughs.
7. The auctioneer asks for bids.
8. The foreigner and snobby lady bid at the same time (angrier and angrier).
9. The old lady mocks them and laughs hysterically.

Try to assess if these sound stories built or told their story in a time span that seemed neither excessively long nor truncated. When the timing is right, a scene can give you a sense of completion. It will be a satisfying experience in which you are with the scene all the way and don't feel unsatisfied when it's over.

Aim: To feel the effect of the different timing of actions.

Exercise 9.14: Stage directions: One student calls out stage directions to the others in the group, who will follow the directions (however many he or she chooses). The stage directions create a story, which the students act out as they are called out. This story can be done over and over at different speeds and levels—using pauses, silences, or neither.

Example: Student says (and others act out):

1. Mary walks nervously into the room.

2. Grandpa is sleeping.

3. Mary accidentally knocks over a chair.

4. Grandpa wakes up and yells at her.

5. Mary walks over to Grandpa and apologizes profusely.

6. She takes hold of Grandpa's hands, begs for forgiveness.

7. She accidentally pulls Grandpa out of the chair.

Example: The student can give stage directions and add lines using dynamics, pauses, and intention. Student says (and others act out):

1. Chuchi and Rocco walk like macho men to the middle of the street.

2. Buck and Cinderblock come in from the opposite side, just as macho.

3. Chuchi points his right forefinger into Cinderblock's face.

4. Chuchi says, "Get outta the way."

5. Cinderblock snorts and puts his hand on Chuchi's shoulder and says, "Who's getting outta whose way?"

6. Rocco steps forward beside Chuchi. Rocco says, "Ha."

7. Buck moves next to Cinderblock and says, "Ha ha."

8. Chuchi and Rocco raise up their chins and clench their fists.

9. Buck and Cinderblock do the same.

10. Angela and Trudy walk by, paying no attention. Couldn't care less.

11. All four guys turn to look at them.

12. All four start making comments toward the girls like:
    "Hey baby. Ooh, what a pretty face."
    "Ain't you a angel. You kill me, girl."
    "Give daddy a smile."
    (and so on)

13. Angela and Trudy turn around for a second and give the guys a look.
    Angela says to the guys, "You're pathetic."
    Trudy laughs.
    They exit.

14. The guys stand there, not knowing what to do for a minute.
    They start slapping hands and punching arms, congratulating one another.

15. Chuchi says, "They loved me, man."

16. Buck says, "That one chick practically had a heart attack over me."

17. Cinderblock says, "Ain't I the devil?"

18. Rocco says, "I'm a vampire. I'm a lady killer."

19. They start praising one another at the same time and stride off all full of themselves.

Aim: To fill a simple moment of time with purpose; to measure emotion and time.

Exercise 9.15: Pick a simple situation. Ask each student or group of students to play it three different ways and at four different speeds. The three ways:

1. In one or two quick movements

2. By discussing it with a friend

3. By telling a story about it

The four speeds:

1. Calmly

2. Taking it with exaggerated patience

3. Frantically

4. In a temper tantrum

Example: Theme: Lost Your Wallet

1. Look at the floor. Urgently pat pockets.

2. "Have you seen my wallet? I've looked all over the place and I can't find it anywhere!"

3. I walked to school today and when I got to the security desk I opened my bag and couldn't find my wallet. This is such a pain because my money and ID were in it.

Can you see how the different speeds use time differently? Each emotional state requires its own sense of time—its own inner speed.

You can choose other speeds to interpret the same theme, including:

1. Speedy and cartoonish

2. In slow motion

3. Talking about it fearfully—making an excuse

4. Using body language that says you don't care

This exercise is valuable as a transition into the act of writing. You are dealing not only with time but with points of view and a choice of tone. Rather than define or explain these categories of writing, it's better to use exercises and let the student learn by self-expression within the exercise.

TEN

MUSIC AND CHOREOGRAPHY

MEX-MONGO

    What is an artiste?

    I don't know.

    Write me a letter, Mr. Picasso.

    Tell me about your spray paints and your subway wall.

    What do you dream, Mr. Chagall?

    I like dirty words.

    I think they look right.

    I paint multicolored curses late at night.

    I make backgrounds of the city,

    In the summer or the snow.

    Is that what you did, Mr. Van Gogh?

    I'd like to paint a sneaker

    A hell of a sneaker

    A big-ass sneaker

    Big as the D train

    And some day, you know

They will build
The Sneaker Subway Memorial Museum
For all of us veterans
Of Police and Graffiti wars.

For all those whose feets got electrified . . .

—Elizabeth Swados and Tony, age seventeen, in *Runaways*

You may or may not want to do a musical or a show with songs. I am a composer, so I write music all the time. But the decision shouldn't be based on whether you as the director can carry a tune or play an instrument. I've worked with directors who can't hold a tune but have an exquisite sense of how to use music, so bear that in mind.

I used to write most of the music for my student shows, setting my students' words or ideas to music. Lately I've found that music has become more organic and accessible to students than it was ten years ago. Perhaps it's the advent of rap, slam poetry, the iPod, or the Internet, but students of every age seem to be plugging earphones into one another's ears, sharing a favorite song or wild instrumental. They bring in their computers and play instruments they discovered on the Web. In my latest student show, I found myself replacing three-quarters of my own songs with students' original compositions.

First of all, students appreciate my music but feel it is somewhat alien to them, and, second, once they get going, they become intoxicated with the power of songwriting. They often don't need me or an adult piano player to help them. (I do work with them on decisions about length and content, however.) Unlike with the other aspects of our theater work, students seem to know *exactly* what they are doing when they choose music. As the students compose their own music, the mood of the room goes from sullen and withdrawn to three-quarters of

the students wanting to take a chance. Often students will help one another out in collaborations and will write songs together. But their musical work requires as much attention as words and movements.

Therefore it's a serious decision whether you want to create your
work with or without music. If you choose to use singing or instrumen-
tals in your show, think about using the following exercises, which I've
found gradually build up confidence and technique. Ironically, the beginning music exercises can be difficult and disagreeable to the emerg-
ing student ensemble. Singing in front of one another seems to be more
humiliating than posing against a wall or reading a monologue. But one
day—maybe two weeks or so into the process—the embarrassment and
self-consciousness seem to disappear and the group sings the music at
exhilarating decibel levels. Often when I arrive at the space, the students are already there, working out their harmonies. The power of
making music liberates untouched inner thoughts and voices.

I try to put the technical vocal work and music work in separate
categories and at different points in the rehearsal. I usually do the
song and music development at the end of a session with the discussions and writing. In truth, there's no real difference, but I separate
them at the beginning so that the students will feel more ownership
when they're singing. Even so, there are certain technical skills that
are both teachable and useful to develop—such as singing in harmony and learning how to arrange an original song. Eventually, any
song has to be made an organic part of the whole piece, which might
affect a song's length or point of view. For this part of the process, I
usually bring in a music director to help translate the spontaneous
a cappella work into a repeatable form.

The music director must not be confused with an uptight music
teacher. He or she should be up on the most recent styles of music
and have a natural feel for the newest rhythms and melodies. The
idea is to capture the students' ideas rather than impose structures or
rules upon them. These exercises can also be used on their own for

anyone who wants to explore musical performance and composition outside the making of a show.

General Music Exercises

Aim: To try to express what is usually instinctive; to hear with words.

Exercise 10.1: Ask each member of the company to bring from home a CD with a song that he or she truly loves. Students should play their favorite songs for the group and explain why they are especially passionate about that particular cut. Make sure that students try to describe what it is in the music that moves them—instead of just saying it's the lyrics or the group or the singer that's performing it. (On the other hand, sometimes students are so moved by lyrics, they may come in and simply want to read them as poetry.) Ask:

1. What are the instruments doing?
2. What is it about the combination of instruments and voices that you respond to? Do you have a favorite instrumental part?
3. At what point in the music does the song move you the most?
4. Talk about what the lyrics say to you.
5. Why are those lyrics important to you in your life now?
6. What is a favorite line or lines of the music and lyrics together?
7. What does the song say to you?

Aim: To take the first steps to songwriting.

Exercise 10.2: Ask the ensemble to choose a song for which they all know the melody. The group sings the melody on *la la la*. Then ask for a topic they can agree on. Work together to set words about the chosen topic to the existing melody.

Example:

    Song: "Satisfaction" (The Rolling Stones)

    Topic: Excellent pizza

    Old lyric: I can't get no—satisfaction

    New lyric: I just love my—slice of pizza

Do this several times and encourage individual students to try their own settings.

Aim: To learn musical styles and fit them to a subject.

Exercise 10.3: The ensemble should select a topic they all agree on, then divide into groups of four or five. Each group should choose a style of music and then go off and set four original lines to that style of music. If possible, the music should be made up: only if students are at a total loss should they continue to use imitations of real songs.

Example: I use rhyme in these examples, but I don't care if my students use it or not. Rhyme can be a gift or it can be an easy way to avoid dealing deeply with a subject.

Topic: Cars

    Group 1: reggae   *Oh, I like my cars* [put music in]
                                     Yes, I love black Cadillacs
                                     With a driver in the front
                                     And a TV in the back

    Group 2: ballad   *Oh, my Honda—a—a* [music]
                                       My beautiful yellow Honda—
                                     I like your funny sha—a—ape
                                     You're like a square flower—

Group 3: hip-hop	*I think*
	Those Volkswagen bugs are the best
	Rolling on the street like a tiny insect
	If you get me a bug, I'll take you where
	Ever you want to go, yes I will take you there
Group 4: blues	*My baby's got a Mustang*
	But she won't let me ride
	My baby's got a Mustang
	But she won't let me ride
	She's hurting my feelings
	And hurting my pride
Group 5: musical theater	*I want to race you to the corner*
	In my beamer
	It moves so smooth and fast it's a dream, sir
	It's real expensive
	But it gleams, sir
	It is lit by perfect moonlight
	Know what I mean, sir?

Aim: To understand how theater music has different uses from generic songs.

Exercise 10.4: Once again, divide the students into smaller groups. Have them set up a short improvisation and create a scene that will "go into a song." (The first time they can use a song they know, just to get used to the idea.) The following examples use existing songs.

Example:

1. Improv: BOY: Welcome home.

   GIRL: Thanks.

BOY: What was it like fighting there?

GIRL: Very hard. Very rough.

BOY: You got hurt, I see.

GIRL: Yes, but I don't need care. I fight for freedom!

Song: *Oh, beautiful for spacious skies*
For amber waves of grain . . . (and so on).

2. Improv: A boy hugs his knees. He's afraid. A girl approaches him, tries to get him to move. He's too afraid. He's locked into his world. The girl leans down to him . . . The girl softly sings . . .

Song: *Baby, Baby, give me your answer true*
I'm half crazy over the likes of you . . . (and so on).

Aim: To combine the creation of a scene with songs so they can work together.

Exercise 10.5: The ensemble should break up into separate groups. Each group should create a scene through improv that leads up to or incorporates an original song of four lines.

Example: A student is a character hoarding a piece of bread. He won't share it with anyone else. They beg; they cry. They are starving, but he still won't give them any bread.

The group sings:

> *Give us what we want*
> *Give us what we need*
> *We are starving*
> *Give us what we want*
> *On the count of three*
> *Or we'll beat you*

> *Or we'll treat*
> *You bad*
> *You sad stingy*
> *Man*
> *One, two, three . . .*

They pile on the selfish character.

Example: The students play characters in a clique. The snobby students are trying to decide whether or not two new girls are cool enough to be allowed into their group.

SALLY: They seem kind of stupid.

JOHN: They dress funny.

ANN: I don't know, they seem kind of sweet.

SALLY: Should we give them a chance?

JOHN: They might bring us down.

ANN: Oh, let's let them hang out with us just this one time.

The clique gestures that the two girls should come along with them.

SALLY and JOHN: Hurry up.

The two outsider girls sing:

> *We don't need you*
> *We don't want you*
> *You're not good people*
> *And we*
> *Only hang with kind and loving souls.*

The clique moves off, surprised and embarrassed.

Aim: To learn to use music as atmosphere and soundscape.

Exercise 10.6: The group becomes an invisible orchestra for a film. One student is the conductor, another is the storyteller or film narrator. The storyteller improvises a narration of a horror story, love story, or any other tale that is big and broad and has a lot of action. The conductor leads the "orchestra," indicating the changing sounds he or she wants from the students with the hands and voice. The conductor listens carefully to the storyteller, and the rest of the students listen to the conductor as they imitate his or her sounds.

Example:

STORYTELLER: It was a dark and stormy night . . .

CONDUCTOR (to orchestra): *ooooooooh*

CHORUS: *ooooooooh*

STORYTELLER: And a kangaroo was hopping along in the heavy rain and winds . . .

CONDUCTOR: *badop badop badop ttttttttttttttttttttttttttttttt ooooooooh*
Kangaroo   rain   wind

CHORUS: *badop badop badop ttttttttttttttttttttttttttttttt ooooooooh*

STORYTELLER: And for some reason, the rain made the kangaroo laugh . . .

CONDUCTOR: *ttttttttttttttttttttttttttttttttttbadop badop badop badop hahahahahahaha*

CHORUS: *ttttttttttttttttttttttttttttttttttttbadop badop badop badop hahahahahahaha*

STORYTELLER: . . . and cry.

CONDUCTOR: *haha awwwnh*

CHORUS: *haha awwwnh*

Exercise 10.7: Sit in a circle. Do the exercise in which one student begins a story and, after a few sentences, passes it on to the next student. This time, however, have each student sing his or her line rather than speak it. The music should be improvised and very simple—you can even have a student sing one note.

Example:

STUDENT 1: (*sings*) You wouldn't believe what I saw today

STUDENT 2: (*sings*) A pineapple in the middle of the street

STUDENT 3: (*sings*) I thought it was going to be crushed so I

STUDENT 4: (*sings*) Called out to the Jack Russell terrier that was sitting drinking coffee . . .

Aim: To make music of every moment and to hear it in every moment.

Exercise 10.8: Name a certain day Opera Day, and during the most mundane activities, have the students sing their conversations. The style of the music doesn't have to be operatic. It can be blues, jazz, rhyme—or any mix of styles.

Example:

LIZ: (*sings*) Good afternoon. I hope you had a good day.

STUDENT 1: (*sings*) Thank you, I did. I aced my Spanish test.

STUDENT 2: (*sings*) My day sucked. My girlfriend and I had a fight.

STUDENT 3: (*sings*) Would anyone like some Doritos?

LIZ: (*speaks*) Okay, let's get to work.

The singing comes and goes in spurts like this throughout the rehearsal. The director signals when it is to come in and out.

Aim: To learn to write for a character; to spark the students' imagination.

Exercise 10.9: Have a discussion about what kind of song a given character or someone in a given situation would sing. Make a list; be specific. How would a certain character feel, talk, sing?

Example:

1. A ditzy girl sings about . . .
   when you're waiting for a phone call.

2. A jock sings about . . .
   having been through a tough time, but he's feeling things might get better. Keep your head up.

3. The one who never finds love sings . . .
   a song about how beautiful a girl or guy is.

4. A braggart who makes up stories sings . . .
   a ballad about his adventures with a friend.

5. You sing about . . .
   being alone and overwhelmed.

6. A pilot sings about . . .
   a time of day and why he loves it.

7. A newscaster sings . . .
   a song about a horrible news item (e.g., the nine-year-old who killed her eleven-year-old best friend).

8. A newscaster sings . . .
   a song about a good news item (e.g., there may be peace for a day in Iraq).

9. A student who's graduating sings about . . .
   how he messed up a relationship with a girl (or guy).

10. The sister of a genius sings about . . .
    longing to be good enough.

11. Two immigrant outsiders sing to . . .
    celebrate friendship.

12. A guy trying to be cool sings . . .
    telling a wild story.

During the time put aside for writing or after rehearsal at home, you
and a partner (or partners) make a song about any of these topics (or
any theme these subjects inspire). Start with the character: how
would he or she sing?

Exercise 10.10: Now start with words or music or both together.

Example: Ditzy girl waits for a phone call. Style: girl punk. First you
create a chorus that's simply and easily repeated:

> *Will he, will*
> *He will he will he*
> *Call me?*
> *Will he, will he . . .*

This chorus goes in between each solo verse; all members of the
group sing it. Each solo verse is made up by the girl who sings it and
presents a new attitude.

> GIRL 1 solo, urgent and loud:
>
> > *Is that the phone?*
> > *Is that the phone?*
> > *Don't nobody get on the phone!*
>
> GIRL 2 solo, longing and wishful:
>
> > *Will he call?*
> > *Will he call?*

> *Do I care?*
> *Do I care?*

GIRL 3 solo, feigning indifference:
> *Do I even know him at all!*

If the words aren't coming to you, go over the line of music again and again until you attach words to the music—even words that don't make sense. Little by little, you'll be able to fill in words that form a coherent thought or image.

If you come up with words but can't find a melody, try saying the words in a rhythm. Speak the words to that simple rhythm, then sing the words on one note. Put in another note. See what happens.

Here are some lyrics written by students for one of my shows (this one is a rap song):

> *If you want a man to do your bidding*
> *And he thinks that your orders might be jive*
> *Slip him some dollars, some drugs or a Porsche*
> *There's nothing that works like a bribe*
>
> *I'm the king of the castle and you're a dirty rascal*
> *I'm the king of the castle and you're a dirty rascal*
>
> *Other young slaves need different encouragement*
> *So you dig in their past, find the trash*
> *Show them old photographs, letters and documents*
> *Blackmail works better than cash*

Aim: To hear music in detail and understand more of its structure.

Exercise 10.11: If possible, have a keyboard player or guitarist visit the rehearsal. Whether the whole group has written one song together or separate partners have come up with a number of songs, have the instrumentalist improvise an accompaniment to each song. The same is true for having a drummer or DJ visit the rehearsal for hip-hop. See how an instrument can change the feel or flow of a song. If your rhythmic sense isn't compatible with what the musician plays behind your song, ask the musician to play how you want. Possible issues:

1. Not rhythmic enough

2. Too many notes

3. Too simple

4. Too heavy

On the other hand, you may want the following:

5. Short jumpy notes (staccato)

6. Long, blending notes (legato)

Aim: To be attuned to listening, even in "real" life.

Exercise 10.12: Found instruments. Keep your ears open outside of rehearsals for objects you think might make good or interesting sounds.

1. Pots and pans

2. Wine bottles

3. A jar of rice

4. The inside of a piano

5. Singing into a mailing tube

6. The blender

7. A basketball being dribbled on a wooden floor

8. Radio static

Aim: To hear more complex music and expand its definition.

Exercise 10.13: Have a session in which the students bring in their found instruments. Each one should be demonstrated in a solo and then put together with others to make a song or noise.

1. See if you want to add some words or vocal sounds to the sounds of the found instruments.
2. See if there is a pattern of repeated sounds that can be sung or chanted along with the strange music. Are there words?

Exercise 10.14: Suggest that students write songs with a melody and words. When a student brings in a song, the group can help arrange it.

1. When is there a solo?
2. When does the chorus come in?
3. Is there harmony?
4. Does it get louder or softer?
5. What happens when you try the song with different rhythms under it?
6. In what way do you want the words to come across? Gentle? Simple? Nasty? Triumphant? Sad? Spooky?

Aim: To go beyond the music, words, and characters of a song to a special performance.

Exercise 10.15: See if a student can write a song for someone else in the group. What is it about the singer's voice that inspires the song? How will the composer make the song fit the singer? You will find that if students do the musical exercises, even if they don't write a complete song, their hearing will become more acute about all music.

CHOREOGRAPHY

I think that in this kind of theatrical work, dancing for dancing's sake should be minimal, unless you are a choreographer and you want to create a show with your students that involves classical, modern, or jazz dance. So I'm going to concentrate on dance movements that come out of the music or drama within an ensemble that is not specifically trained in any dance. Therefore, I will assume, as with everything else in this book, that the dance or movement is made with this particular group of students in mind—and is shaped by their sensibility. Here are three choices:

1. You have a separate choreographer who observes the workshops and then comes in and teaches steps and formations.

2. You use different volunteer choreographers within your own group and then supervise them.

3. You have the group create dances together. The choreographer or director can help them organize and clean up their work.

I've used all three methods, but for the sake of this book, I will concentrate on the second and third methods. I want to be able to come up with movement or dancing that reflects the students' body language. Since my sessions are not dance classes, I avoid trying to inspire students to be expert in step combinations or athletic leaps. If I have one or two "real dancers" in my group, then I usually ask them to create dances for themselves. Or we create one together, but I don't insist that others take part.

General Dance Exercises

Aim: To hear music through the body and the imagination.

Exercise 10.16: You have chosen for your students one of the songs
created, adapted, or preexisting for your music. Send the ensemble
off in separate groups and instruct each group to take two different
eight-bar—or four-bar, sixteen-bar, whatever you choose—parts of
the song and come up with specific steps (or use a simple repeating
chorus). When the ensemble gets back together, have each group
perform its steps. They should repeat them as many times as necessary so that they remember them throughout the immediate rehearsal period. After all the presentations are completed, you will see
that many groups have chosen the same parts of the song to choreograph. Make sure they remember what they did.

Exercise 10.17: Form new groups. Assign each group a different part
of the song that hasn't yet been choreographed. The groups should
choreograph the new part of the song and then reconvene. At this
point, you will have several ideas of steps for each part of the song.
You can choose from these separate choreographed pieces and make
a dance that is a kind of quilt of the students' separate inventions—or
you might add a step or two of your own to define and strengthen the
existing combination.

THE STUDENTS CAN BE active in helping you choose the right
steps for the song out of their own work. I have found that students
are selfless and will often suggest other students' steps for the right
place in the dance. But if you can't find a set of steps that fits a section
of the song, you can make them up together on the spot. Steps and
gestures for choruses of the song in which the whole group dances often get choreographed spontaneously. The director should keep his
or her eye open for the one step that might define all the rest. Once
everyone has learned all the steps and gestures to the entire song, you

can begin to hand out solos, duets, and trios to the students who really want to do them and will practice the steps outside of rehearsal.

We used this process to create the group dances in *Runaways*. The resulting dances were fresh and organic and almost entirely choreographed by the nineteen members of the cast. In fact, we got a Tony nomination for choreography!

It's important for the students to realize that not all dances have to be made up of conventional kicks, turns, and steps. For instance, I had a boy in *Runaways* who was a genius on the skateboard. Not only could he do all the tricks that go along with the sport, but he could use the skateboard with unusual grace and lyricism. When we had to choreograph a song about leaving and loss, he found moves that matched the melancholy of the song—while still staying true to skateboard technique.

I had another young actor who had a brown belt in martial arts. He made a fierce but graceful fight dance for *The Hating Pot* (a show about racism and anti-Semitism). We also made a dance that transitioned from Jewish hora to hip-hop to the punk pogo and then combined all three. We staged a gang war in *The Violence Project* that was done entirely in rhythmic stepping, clapping, and stomping.

Aim: To expand the definition of dance.

Exercise 10.18: Ask each student to think of an activity that isn't a dance, but could be performed to celebrate the movement of the body.

Examples (these should be done to music):

1. A football scrimmage
2. Bouncing a soccer ball off knee to head to elbow
3. Playing catch

4. Doing double Dutch jump rope

5. Imitating a cat, lion, chimpanzee, fish

6. Carrying a basket on the head or a child on the shoulders

7. Working on a production line in a factory

8. Standing on line for food

9. Marching in a band or army formation

10. Boxing

11. Swinging on a rope or swing

12. Playing an instrument

13. Doing a rope trick

14. Using a bicycle

Aim: To enhance imagination and connectivity.

Exercise 10.19: Pick an unusual object and dance with it as if it's a live partner.

Examples:

1. A broom

2. A chair

3. A garbage can

4. A boom box

5. An empty cardboard box

6. A piece of clothing

7. One shoe

Exercise 10.20: Find an unexpected place for dancing.

Examples:

1. On a piano
2. Standing on a chair
3. Standing on a table
4. Crouched under a table
5. In a supermarket
6. Stepping through a crowd of people

Exercise 10.21: Pick a character and dance like him or her.

Examples:

1. A troll
2. An alien
3. A drunk
4. A fussy old lady
5. Frankenstein's monster
6. A cartoon character
7. A living vegetable

Then put together two unrelated characters and see how their dances change each other.

Exercise 10.22: Gather in a circle and create a circle dance, facing in and watching whoever leads the steps as you move around.

Examples:

1. Dancing on the heels, dancing on the toes
2. Bending the knees
3. Circling with one foot, then the other

Exercise 10.23: Create a square dance where the "caller" calls out unusual steps and movements.

Examples:

1. Honor your partner. Honor your corner. Pinch your partner's nose.
2. Do-si-do and swing to the left. Swing to the right. Swing up and down.
3. Now let's go to the door and back.
4. Let's dance backward like a chicken.

THE DANCE WORK IS active and challenging but shouldn't be torture to anyone. If you have a couple of students (and it won't always be boys) who simply can't pick up steps, give them one or two movements that go with the music and have them repeat the movements over and over. This way they can have the joy of moving to music without the humiliation of not being able to tell their left feet from their right.

ELEVEN

PUTTING A SHOW TOGETHER

LAZAR:

Hey, hey,

Who is directing this movie?

The sound track is all wrong, all wrong.

It's too gloomy. It's too savage.

We need some violins.

Something more upbeat.

People will not wait in line for two hours unless they can go out
humming something upbeat.

And who is editing this thing?

It's all choppy and black and white.

Nothing is black and white.

We need some Technicolor, or Vistavision,

Some Sensurround.

What this movie needs is a hero.

But there are no more heroes.

Do you know why there are no more heroes?

It's because when George Washington decided to found this
country,

He went to Washington, D.C.,

Which at that time was swarming with superheroes.

There were so many superheroes, he had to get rid of them so
    that he could build the Capitol.

So he rented a printing press,

And he lured all the superheroes into the printing press,

And he flattened them out. Just flattened them out.

And that's why there are D.C. comics.

It's all those flattened-out superheroes stapled together.

And there were so many that they had to build the Library of
    Comics.

And I have evidence. I have proof.

The Spectacular Spiderman, flattened out.

Superman, flattened out.

The Incredible Hulk, flattened out.

Every superhero is flattened out.

And now it's time to tap dance.

—David, age nineteen, in *Runaways*

It's difficult to gather all the elements—the workshops, the discussions, the writing, the music, the movement, and of course the acting—to finally put together a play. And though this is a book about the theater, you may notice I don't have a separate chapter on acting. That is because I believe that by now the students will be fluent in the vocabulary of the show, understand its separate parts, and be prepared to perform, both as an ensemble and as individual participants. All these different kinds of preparation have unconsciously made them actors. Now they can work on applying their skills to the piece of work that has been developing along with their skills.

    What is the order of the show? Does it have a narration, a plot? Does it use image, scene, and song in an abstract way—like a music video? Does it have a lot of movement? Is it mostly spoken? Is it non-verbal? These are the decisions you've been making all along as you measure your company's strength, energy, and expertise. You are putting together an orchestra and each instrument is unique in its character and the mood it evokes. You know your students well by now and you see their range and power. You look back and see that a "casting" process has been going on all the time.

Though your stylistic choice may differ, there are certain essential parts of the whole that have to be considered in any theatrical piece. The first is the order. Where do you put this monologue or that movement piece? How long is this scene and will what comes next be shorter or longer? I think a great deal about the Greek plays I did with Andrei Serban. In each play the tension was played out with an excruciating sense of dynamics and timing; moments were held for just so long—stretched to their limit—and then *boom*: like a downpour, the release came. When Jason and Medea met face to face, they were whispering their venomous accusations at each other, their voices slowly rising in volume and consonants becoming sharper. You could feel the air between them stretching like the head of a drum, followed by a crash and a *bam* from the percussion. The audience would jump, startled, and the drums would begin to play ominous rolls as the two characters let out the rage they'd been keeping inside for so long. I would write down the order of sounds like this:

1. Whispered section
2. Sharp syllables, still quiet
3. Long tense pulling sounds
4. Voices tighter and tighter
5. Boom from timpani
6. Vicious animalistic screeching
7. Empty and quiet

Sometimes the actors would try another order. For instance, the scene could start with the hit on the timpani and Jason and Medea screaming violently at each other, breaking like thunder into the room. Then they could bring their voices down lower and lower in the dead quiet of a murderous rage. Silence could be used for mockery or the low roll of the drum could underscore a cold threat. Now the order would be:

1. Boom from timpani
2. Vicious animal screeching
3. Voices tight, changing gradually into . . .
4. Long pulling sounds
5. Sharp syllables (quiet)
6. Intense whispering
7. Silence

Would this work as well? In order to feel the perfect progression within a work, you can only try, test, and redo until like puzzle pieces everything falls into place.

When I look for expertise in creating an order I also study the Beatles album *Sgt. Pepper's Lonely Hearts Club Band*. Though it has no real plot, the music nonetheless flows from one song to another as if it is taking us through a story. The story isn't linear, but we follow the band through a musical journey that has its own loose relationship. I've always admired this album and think it has a mysterious quality that may just result from the songs' being in the right order. The Who's rock opera *Tommy* has a little more of a conventional plot but it is still moved forward by the order of the songs.

A PIECE ABOUT SURVIVAL

The first musical I did in New York was called *Nightclub Cantata*. It was a cabaret made up of an unusual mix of elements. I was attempting to open up the form, make it more theatrical and surprising, so I set the words of poets to music: Sylvia Plath, Frank O'Hara, Pablo Neruda, and Muriel Rukeyser. The musical settings ranged from calypso to blues to Indian raga; I even included rhythmic bird chants from Africa. *Nightclub Cantata* was made up of all this as well as a kind of rap in Hebrew and a sung rendition of Delmore Schwartz's short story "In Dreams Begin Responsibilities." As random as these pieces may sound, they nonetheless made a kind of real sense to me. I saw them all as parts of a theater piece about the extreme challenges we face in life, and how we meet them and somehow survive. I hoped to present a life that is worth the fight for survival, because if you survive, there is still humor, beauty, and even love to be sought.

The key to making *Nightclub Cantata* work was its inner rhythms and how the tension could be portrayed without narration. Since I desired to create a piece about survival, I knew I had to make a graph of emotional intensity that had to start with the growing terrors that one had to survive. The graph would look something like the one on page 244. Bear in mind that although the description is dark, humor was an essential part of the mix.

Then the young actors and I proceeded to place separate poems and songs throughout the musical according to each category. We asked ourselves what the musical energy was of each section, so that we'd discover when and where to move on. Which piece moved the theme to a more intense energy? How could we avoid staying in one place? How could we create surprise without making emotional non sequiturs—jumping from one emotional texture to another simply because the *sound* of the piece seemed to work? At the same time,

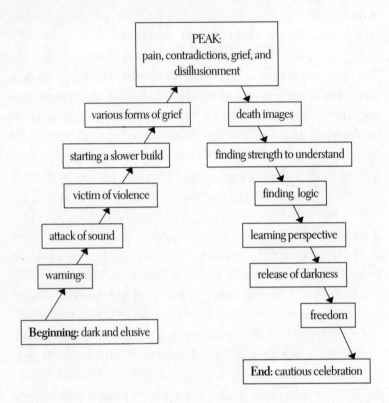

I tried to figure out how to create inexplicable jumps in the cantata that could be shocking or funny. This is where I relied on my artistic instinct. It's the kind of situation in which no two directors or writers would map out the same progression.

When I work with students, I include them in the creation of such an order so that they can live through a progression rather than simply visualizing it. But before we work on the final order of a show, we all practice using the following exercises.

General Progression Exercises

Aim: To learn to sense nonverbal progression.

Exercise 11.1: Each student finds two songs—contemporary or any other—that he or she believes are theatrical. He or she should also find two poems, paragraphs, or scenes, or write monologues, that have a relationship to the songs. He or she should place them in an order that makes sense musically and emotionally. The connections may not be obvious, but the student should be able to explain why he or she chose this order.

Example (from *Nightclub Cantata*):

1. "Dibarti ati allera"— a duet in Hebrew (performed by two actors) that is a fight between a man and a woman. It builds to a ferocious confrontation.

2. "In Dreams Begin Responsibilities"—a short story (performed by the whole company) set in a gentle, humorous ragtime mode. The story is about a boy who dreams he is in a movie theater on his twenty-first birthday watching his parents courting. (Are the lovers in the first piece setting up the unhappy marriage in the plot of the second piece?)

3. "Are You with Me"—a quiet, ironic jazz ballad (performed by one actor). The singer is asking an invisible partner if he's in for the long haul or is he going to get up and go.

4. "Raga"—a lively dance with sticks set in a row on the floor. The actors sing a note and jump to where it is on imaginary piano keys separated by the sticks. The movie *Big* contains a scene that uses a similar technique. The group creates a melody by running up and down the line of sticks while others stay put and sing a droning note over and over. The idea is to keep the pitches correct and not step on any note you're not supposed to sing.

Here is my emotional logic:

Scene	Style	Progression of cantata
1. "Dibarti" — a man and woman having a vicious fight. (Hebrew has many sharp knife-like sounds.) Building speed and pitch.	Fast tempo. Two voices with percussion and staccato	A fight
2. "In Dreams" — a quiet meditation on whether or not a boy's parents were actually right for each other. This reflects back on the fight which came before. It is the child feeling the animosity of his parents.	The whole company at a moderate speed, with a ragtime nostalgic feel	An unhappy marriage that produces an unhappy son
3. "Are You with Me" — one singer's asking an unknown love about his loyalty. A lone person under a spotlight. This slows down the pace, isolates a person, and can reflect back the child's melancholy about his parents.	A jazz solo — very slow and modest, frank, ironic, and with a rich melody	The isolation and mistrust of someone who's been hurt
4. "Raga" — a break in mood. Going to something strenuously athletic that is fun and skillful. But there's also the underlying tension of "if you step on a crack, you break your mother's back." Can the actor get through this without making a mistake?	Starts slow (from tempo and the song before), and then speeds into a frenzy. Bodies and voices very active.	You can't dwell in the past, but have to jump into the present and take risks.

Aim: Learning how one moment affects another.

Exercise 11.2: Break the group into smaller ones and have each sub-group take four pieces from a familiar show—any four. Find an order, and perform it for the larger group.

Example: Pieces from *Runaways*

1. Chant in spoken Spanish. A woman screaming at another that she's a whore.

2. Song of the child prostitute—a very quiet, eerie two-note chant, like a monologue, in which a young girl talks about her life.

3. The first chant comes back, but this time with nineteen voices, mocking and threatening the woman; the sound is extremely dangerous and violent. It peaks and she is thrown on the floor.

4. One second of silence. The comic character of Lazar comes in wearing a tuxedo and taps with a briefcase, breaking the whole mood and talking about comic books and saying that superheroes are "flattened out."

The child prostitute song and the violence that follows are superseded by Lazar's tap dance as an intentional non sequitur. The play gets extremely dark and the audience (as well as the young actors) must be brought back to lighter perspectives or the play will become a dirge. Also, thematically speaking, for every lost child who is destroyed, there's another doing his best to understand his unpredictable life. (Even if he has to lodge a complaint about the failure of superheroes to show up.) And finally, I never wanted to lose track of the fact that the victims are children. Thus the comic book.

As you experiment and take note of the order within one section, you will begin to see a flow for the entire play that you'll then try to make "perfect." This is one of the most difficult jobs. You will have to order and reorder and make many cuts and rewrites. If cuts are required, I ask my students to write anonymously on a piece of paper what songs or scene they think we can get rid of. One or two pieces are usually clear candidates for the ax; others are more of a struggle. From the first day, I let students know that some of their work may be cut. I remind them constantly. Even so, they experience the hurt of rejection. But they recover more quickly than the student who hasn't been warned and who hasn't been told it's nothing personal. Cutting a monologue or some lines to a song is not a statement about a person's competence or lovability. This has to be made clear so you can be ruthless in your decision making. I have had to cut roughly half the songs and monologues in most of the plays I've done. My colleagues and I have whole scores of cut songs that either get used in another show or are never seen or heard from again.

Let's say you've found an order, or an emotional map that suits you. You and your students are now in a more conventional rehearsal period; the moment for live performance is not too far ahead. Words should be memorized, initial blocking done. You believe that without too many changes, your show is complete. At this point I start to pay attention to transitions. It is said that directing is all about transitions, and I know that I concentrate as much on the action in between scenes as on the action within a scene itself. I've witnessed perfectly good work falling apart because not enough attention was paid to these essential "in between" moments. The workshop exercises you did covering the follow-through to the end of a movement or sound are relevant to the work on transitions. Ideally, students should be aware of every possible moment from the center of the action to a turn to walk offstage. If the concentration lets up, then energy leaks out from the performance. If energy leaks out during too many small transitions, the whole piece starts to deflate. The piece becomes a house of bricks held together by weak mortar. It won't be able to stand up for long.

Transitions have to have meaning—they have to be defined. The students should feel as committed to them as they do to acting characters. The right transitions bring more clarity to what comes before and after as well as to the whole arc of your show.

General Transition Exercises

Aim: To create awareness during transitions.

Exercise 11.3: Put two moments of a play together and have each actor "narrate" what is happening between the two moments.

Example: "I have finished my song. I walk quickly, concentrating on getting offstage. Then I push the table, using my whole body to express the importance of my job. Then I get off really fast, opening up the stage for Sally's scene."

Example: "We've just finished the scene with a shout of victory. As the shout echoes in the air, I use that energy to turn around and take my place on the bench. I sit on the bench but I am too excited, and this propels me to jump up and join in on the chorus of Max's song."

Aim: To learn transitions as primary action and then learn to stay alert for them.

Exercise 11.4: The same exercise, only this time an actor standing in the house speaks to the others who are onstage while the action is going on.

Example:

1. Tim stands up in the audience as John finishes his speech. Everyone walks on from offstage tearfully, as if they're scared to

go out in public. Tim now has the power. Each actor seeks a place where he or she can hide, and the group whispers, "Who's watching me?" After the song, each actor is still afraid and backs up toward the middle of the stage, not knowing the others are all there, so that everyone slams into everyone else, screaming with surprise.

2. Tim picks Laura and, becoming the director, says to her, "Finish your monologue and sit down quietly as if you've said what you need to and you're relieved."

Aim: To quicken reactions, sharpen impulses, and memorize the order of a show.

Exercise 11.5: The actors stand in a circle. One person calls out the name of a scene. An actor rushes to the position of that scene and begins to act it. After the scene is done, he or she rushes back to the circle, and someone else calls out the name of another scene so that the group takes its place for that particular scene. This is good for acquiring a feel for impulse—the energy with which to begin a moment.

Aim: To learn that the end of a movement gives energy to the one that follows.

Exercise 11.6: The actors go through a scene. At the end of the scene, instead of saying the last word, they shout, "Over!" And from the energy of the word "Over!" they transition into the next scene.

Example:

Scene 1:

> JACK: Mary's not going to cut it.
> SANDY: Yeah? Why not?

JACK: Because it's time to show a little loyalty.

SANDY: Fifty dollars is loyalty.

JACK: I don't care about you giving me stuff. I want to hang out.

SANDY: We can hang out spending money.

JACK: You have a one-track OVER!

Scene 2:

> *Glory glory hallelujah*
> *Glory glory hallelujah*
> *Glory glory hallelujah*
> *The truth keeps marching OVER!*

Aim: To explore the show from another point of view.

Exercise 11.7: The group goes through the entire show, but acts only the transitions.

Example:

1. The group marches through the house onto the stage and puts the chairs in position.

2. Rushing, the actors push the chairs to the side of the stage to create a place for John to make his announcement.

3. Lois walks slowly to where John has spoken and looks up to him with admiration.

4. The boys push John to the door. They are impatient.

5. Zack, Leah, and Tom push on the office furniture as if they're beginning a day at work and quickly take their seats.

Aim: To learn the show and stay focused to the end.

Exercise 11.8: Run through the show quickly and without stopping. No breaks or hesitations. This is a common exercise that should be done for any show.

Example: An actor sitting at the front of the stage sings the first line and the last line of her song. After the last line, the students move to where they should go for the next scene. The first line of the scene is all that's said—then the actors jump to the last line of the scene, and from the last line of that scene to the first line of the next scene, and so on.

Aim: To sharpen the memory and learn to re-create acting values at any dynamic, using speed throughout.

Exercise 11.9: Go through the entire show from beginning to end, leaving nothing out, at the fastest possible speed. Nothing should be skipped or done halfway.

Strengthening the Show

Aim: To deepen knowledge of your show and character.

Exercise 11.10: If you have time and the curiosity, see if you can go through four or five scenes backward. (The dialogue or words would be impossible to say backward, so just try to reverse the order of movements and speeches in each scene.)

Exercise 11.11: Pick one or two scenes and have the actors play one another's characters. (I ask my students to know the whole show.)

Exercise 11.12: If the show isn't too long and you have the luxury of time, do two run-throughs back to back, with one whispered and one at regular volume.

Exercise 11.13: If the weather permits, take the students outside and run sections of the show in a radically different setting. They will have to be creative to adapt to the new space.

Exercise 11.14: Do several scenes in a row, asking the students to play them in different styles or emotions from what you've settled on for the show.

IF YOU INSTILL a sense of fun and gamesmanship into rehearsals, the students will learn to work more thoroughly and gain a real sense of true ownership.

THE PERFORMANCE, THE AUDIENCE, AND THE AFTERMATH

Before the first performance in front of an audience, I do exercises to help actors learn how to hold their focus onstage, creating extreme versions of what might happen to them.

Aim: To learn how to hold focus.

Exercise 11.15: One actor stands on the stage and performs a mono-logue or song while the others sit in the audience and talk to one another. Can the actor keep going?

Exercise 11.16: One actor stands on the stage performing and a heck-ler from the back row calls out insults—"You stink," "Go back to the farm," and so on. Can the actor keep his or her composure?

Exercise 11.17: Two or three actors do a scene. One purposely forgets his lines and stops talking. How do the others cover for him?

Exercise 11.18: Ask the students to do their scene bumping into furniture and dropping props, while never losing the pace or intention of the scene.

Exercise 11.19: The cast is onstage for a group moment—maybe a song. Someone yells "Fire!" and the whole cast has to dash out of the theater and then come back in, take their places, and pick up from where they left off as if nothing had happened.

THESE EXERCISES ARE fun and will help students keep perspective on what might seem like disasters during a performance.

I'd like to stress the importance of a warm-up before any performance. This is a time to focus, get the body limber, and open up the voice. It's the time when the student gets in touch with his or her training, both physical and mental. Even more important, it's the time the company comes together and becomes a single force. You've seen football teams huddle together before a game—this isn't much different.

Theater companies all over the world have different kinds of warm-ups. In New York there's a group—Great Jones Repertory—that's been working together on and off for twenty years. They go through a series of vigorous exercises, make sounds, and sing a song, and then Ellen Stewart, who is their director, brings them together in a circle. This group is composed of actors from all over the world. Over the years they've lost some crucial members to AIDS and other diseases, young people who've died before their time. Ellen asks the company to hold hands, and together they chant the names of the lost. They say the names, not with grief, but as if they'll be joining the ensemble for that night's performance. Their spirits are brought into consciousness. After that quiet moment, the company sings a rhythmic song from their show in order to build up power. You can see them becoming revved up, like boxers before a fight. Then they go to their places in complete silence, ready to begin.

Your warm-ups will depend a great deal on songs and exercises that have become precious to you over the rehearsal period. Here are some examples of what might be included in a warm-up. Depending on how much time you have, you can do a thorough session or pick one exercise that gets the group going:

1. Stretching, individually or with a partner

2. Chanting, individually or with a partner

3. Going over lines as a vocal exercise—alone or with a partner

4. Jumping up and down through the space

5. Running around the space, making loud sounds

6. Passing sounds and movements back and forth, as the tempo gets faster and faster

Group warm-up (you can choose from this list or make your own):

1. Running around in a tight circle with a leader who changes steps and speeds

2. Standing in a circle, passing a sound around as if it's an object, changing speeds

3. Passing a clap around the circle, changing speeds

4. Trading moves and rhythms back and forth with a leader

5. If you have songs, singing one song quietly, listening carefully to all the rhythms

6. Taking the same song and shouting part of it

7. Having each student vocalize a long sustained wail that starts at the bottom and increases in pitch and volume until the highest sound is squeezed out, then returns to the bottom (like a siren — up and down)

8. Whispering different speeches and scenes simultaneously to create a cacophony of voices. Listening to the music of the whispers. Bringing the volume up slowly to a shout

9. Taking one another's hands. Bowing heads or lifting heads. Being silent for a moment

10. Singing, chanting, or shouting a favorite moment from the show with the intention of building up the energy — and cheering for yourselves

11. Maintaining absolute silence for at least a minute

I try to instill perspective about the audiences for whom my nervous actors will be performing. Here's some of what I attempt to communicate:

1. Be more scared of me than of the audience.

2. Remember that it's your show, and you already know it's good.

3. Bear in mind that audience reactions can be extremely arbitrary. A playgoer can eat too many dumplings and get a stomachache that makes him dislike what he's seeing, for example.

4. Do you always like what your friends wear? Remember that people have different tastes.

5. Think about the fact that you wouldn't want to have a long dinner with half of the audience (especially the adults). So why do you care what they think?

6. Actors can measure whether they're doing well by the instincts instilled in them over the weeks of rehearsal and performance. Excellence is not measured by an applause-o-meter.

7. Think of all the hours and days we've spent together. Each day was its own show. The process is the gift.

8. Don't lose your sense of community. Work off of each other as a team.

Of course, these words of wisdom barely break through the wall of terror. Unfortunately, our culture is focused on winning, praise, awards, and labels. Our students are steeped in showbiz, gossip shows, stars, and riches. (I will be surprised if, by the time this book is published, there isn't a reality show about high school students struggling to make a play.) Hopefully, the work you've done will sustain your students after the stage fright wears off.

I worry for my students when they perform in front of audiences, but I've never had a group fail to come through. I've watched the students discover their own hidden talents and go deeper and more freely into the moments that make their show. I root for them, knowing that they are out there in front of parents and friends. I see performing for those who know you as thrilling but terrifyingly revealing. And as much as I enjoy audiences who are courteous and respectful of theater etiquette, I am fascinated by my students' sense of duty, even survival, in front of wilder audiences—such as those often found at public schools, juvenile facilities, public hospitals, and nursing homes. I tell them they have to be artistic gladiators. My satisfaction comes when I watch a group of my students perform well and astonish the similar kids in the audience who until that moment didn't even know or care what theater was. There's a kind of secret communication that goes on between the performers and an audience made up of gangs of adolescents as they pass energy back and forth. Theater becomes a rock concert—or perhaps more appropriately, a football game. When the exchange is especially passionate, there is very little space for adults. The work is at its best when the students take over.

Even so, there are some rules. The following guidelines have helped my students handle the inevitable crises:

1. If a student audience is too out of control, the entire cast is to lie down on their backs on the floor of the stage until the audience calms down. (I saw Bette Midler do this once at Radio City Music Hall and thought it was a brilliant tactic.)

2. You are in a musical duet with the audience, so give them time to laugh and clap—but not too much time. (Then you leak energy.)

3. If there's a single heckler, don't stop and don't answer.

4. When things are thrown on the stage, step over them or toss them out of the way. Don't throw them back.

5. The pace of the show is part of what gives it its character. Don't wait for reactions.

6. Don't expect any two audiences to be the same. Try not to expect a laugh one day because you got one the day before. Each audience is totally different from the next.

7. Silence doesn't necessarily mean an audience doesn't like your work. Play the show with the same energy and open spirit as before. I've seen shows where audiences do nothing the whole night—neither laugh nor applaud—and then at the end stand and cheer.

8. Never crack up onstage. Not only do you show that you're immature, but you break the special reality you have created, and then the audience knows you're just actors.

9. During your curtain call, applaud your audience; they've worked hard too.

10. Everyone must always help set up, take down, move, and carry.

11. Don't let the attention go to your head, but don't dismiss what's happened either. You've just had a rare experience in which life has become extremely vivid.

Here are some rules that apply especially to in-school performances for teachers, friends, and parents:

1. Never go onstage displaying an angry or sad mood unless the drama or character calls for it. And even then don't mix personal problems with the job at hand.

2. Don't peek outside the curtain to see who's there or wave; you're trying to create magic.

3. Try not to perform differently when you know someone important is in the audience. This often causes you to push— become too loud or too fast—or to ignore your fellow actors.

4. Don't despair if there are only five people in the audience. As the Talmud says, "You touch one person, you touch the world."

5. Don't try to be better, louder, or more talented than your fellow actors. If someone sticks out, he or she hurts the whole show and comes off as obnoxious.

6. Remember that your loyalty is to the ensemble. Remember how hard you've worked together. Listen for them; watch for each other from the corner of your eye.

7. Concentrate on the present. The timing, the transitions, the characters, the harmonies—make each performance a tribute to all your hard work.

8. Realize that you're privileged—enjoy the fact that you're giving energy and light to others.

9. Each performance is a holiday. Treasure the time and the others who are sharing it with you.

If you are doing more than one performance, make sure the group meets after each show if time allows. Once the audience has left, sit quietly in a circle and discuss the night's (or the afternoon's) work. This isn't a time for criticism and scolding; instead, it is a quiet time when you can analyze what worked and what didn't. And you can laugh about the mistakes or, if necessary, talk over concentration and energy problems individually or as a group. This is also a time to celebrate the triumph of getting through a show, which in itself is a measure of accomplishment in its own right.

This is how I see the process of giving notes, or postperformance critiques, to actors. The students can speak about their individual experiences and problems and talk to me, but, as I've said, I don't allow any student to criticize another in front of the group. If anyone is disgruntled, I give them time alone to vent their frustration and make adjustments for worries that are real.

I believe that notes have to be absolutely truthful, but they should not be angry. Mistakes during performances are natural, but they shouldn't be ignored. For their own sakes, students should know when they can do better—and usually do. I give my notes to everybody at the same time. Humor is essential, but specificity is the best approach for me. Why did the focus go? Where were you when everybody else was singing? Finland? I think your monologue was too fast—did you want to get home early? Plus many variations in that area—that entrance was late, you spoke too softly, why did your character suddenly have an Italian accent? Sometimes I have to ask students if they remember why we're doing the work we do. I have to remind them of the seriousness of the craft and their unspoken deal with themselves, me, and the audience.

If someone is messing up badly, I catch them before they leave the theater and ask what outside our work is causing problems. School? Home? Exhaustion? Friends? On the other hand, if someone is doing especially well, I walk up to that person and say, "Wow, I can really see you growing. You're working hard. It's totally paying off." No "genius"; no "brilliant"; no "You're going to be a star." That scares a student and makes them feel they have to live up to a different standard.

If the whole group does an exceptionally stunning job, no one has to tell them. Fists go up in the air and hips get bumped, hands get shaken forward and backward and palms slapped. Then it's more than a well-done job. The students have worked hard and learned a whole new language. They're clearheaded. They will become autonomous. At this point, I'll step out of the way; the work is theirs.

There's bound to be a letdown during the days that follow the closing. And that's why I try to avoid scheduling performances on the last day of the ensemble's time together. As the adrenaline drops, the students experience both satisfaction and emptiness. But since the work is about more than engaging with audiences, there are exercises that can bring the focus back from applause and roses to the present as well as to ideas for the future.

Postperformance Discussion in a Seated Circle

Aim: To bring the show back to the sacred space and out of the realm of the auditorium and stage.

Exercise 11.20: Each member of the group picks a favorite moment from the show and asks the students who performed in it to re-create it.

Example:

SHAWN: I really love the way Lily sings her solo. I'd like to hear it again. I want to hear her voice. (*Lily stands up or stays seated in the circle and sings the song.*)

LOUISE: I want to do the country-and-western line dance again. It's so powerful. (*The whole group reconfigures into a line and dances.*)

Aim: To reclaim each moment.

Exercise 11.21: Each student describes a moment when he or she was most scared and reenacts it.

Exercise 11.22: Each student recalls a mistake he or she made and reenacts it.

Exercise 11.23: Each student is asked to name a favorite exercise or moment from the whole workshop process and puts the group into physical positions to re-create it.

Exercise 11.24: The group sings an old song that's either been cut or that was used only as an exercise.

Exercise 11.25: Students admit lapses of concentration during the show and display and narrate what went on in their heads.

Example:

1. Sally shows how she was supposed to creep like a spider behind Michael and then put one hand on his shoulder in a menacing gesture.

SALLY: I was afraid that his shoulder was going to be all sweaty and gross.

2. John shows how he was supposed to cross in slow motion across the whole stage like the ghost of memory.

JOHN: I was thinking that I had to go to the bathroom so badly—but would I ever get there?

Aim: Detoxify bad moments.

Exercise 11.26: Have each student re-create a moment of doubt that he or she had during the workshop process.

Example:

TIM: When we were singing the first time I thought, "I gotta get out of here, we sound like a bunch of sick seals."

MARY: The first time I saw James move, I thought, I better stay on this dude's good side or he's gonna kill me.

Aim: To bring students back to the initial motivation.

Exercise 11.27: If you have created an issue-oriented show, have a discussion about the most important issue and what's happening now. Hopefully, the students have not ceased reading and keeping informed.

Example: If your show was about domestic violence, talk about new cases and laws, real stories, and help organizations. What would you add to the show, given what you know now?

Aim: To demonstrate that they can go on—and find new dreams.

Exercise 11.28: Discuss what issues and stories you'd like to do if the group could continue and create a new show.

Aim: To get the imagination into a creative mode.

Exercise 11.29: The group breaks up into smaller groups, and each creates the first scene for a new show.

Aim: To introduce the idea that the students can make theater without you.

Exercise 11.30: Encourage the students to create ensembles of their own and suggest venues for student-initiated work, envisioning a festival of student work.

Exercise 11.31: Discuss what practical steps would have to be taken for students to form ensembles outside school, the way they do rock bands.

YOUR STUDENTS SHOULD LEAVE this experience hungry to make shows even better than the one in which they participated. They'll lead their own versions of games and exercises and experiment with original themes. I have been invited to several student-initiated nights of theater and have witnessed excellent, specific, offbeat work. These visits to garages, street fairs, living rooms, backyards, and basements give me hope that the theater will survive and change and reflect a growing energy rather than a fading past.

TWELVE

MENTORING

AS WITH any theatrical production, close bonds are made among students who have gone through drama classes together or put on a show. The heightened moments and sharing of intense energy create a feeling of having experienced a special adventure together. When students see one another and frequently work together, they create a unique family. They end up feeling affection toward other students they'd never have thought twice about otherwise, and the experience of this togetherness can create lifelong friendships and collaborations. Or as happens in professional theater, these intense friendships prove transitory and individuals go on to a new show and a new family.

I try to keep groups of students together for at least two years. Practically speaking, we've spent so much time developing an ensemble vocabulary and style that it would be a shame to let the artistic camaraderie we've achieved come to an end. I've worked with some groups for three or four years, replacing those that go to college while simultaneously bringing in new, inexperienced students to join us. If we are performing a show that had been completed before, I want to see the experienced students teaching the dances, songs, and staging to those who've recently joined the group. I'm so encouraged when I see the veterans being calm and patient with the others. They remember their own training in great detail, and I know that the eager authority they display is a sign that the work has done its job. Therefore, I purposely give the new recruits over to mentors who might be shorter or younger but who nonetheless know their stuff.

I'm not interested in my students' becoming theater professionals, famous actors, or writers. I care most about the way in which each student has changed and acquired new passions. In the last thirty years, the individuals from my ensembles have spread out in a huge range of occupations. Despite my hesitancy, I've had a number of my students turn out to be movie stars, theater stars, jazz musicians, singers, and stand-up comedians; several others have become directors and founders of rock-and-roll bands. Some of my students have actually gone on to create their own theater groups, and some have become published poets who run their own series in a downtown club. There are those who write books or plays. Others have made choices to work on the business side of the arts as producers, managers, casting directors, or fund-raisers. There are several who teach the arts in school and community settings. And there's always a percentage who continue on as actors, doing the best they can to keep working in an impossible life.

Of course, the majority of my students don't end up in the arts at all. They may instead become psychologists, computer programmers, yoga instructors, professors, teachers, stockbrokers, bartenders, waitresses, or dog walkers. Their choice of profession has a lot to do with where they are in their development. As you can calculate, I have alumni ranging from those in their thirties to those from my most current show who are nine, ten, and eleven. Some are starting to dig into their lives; many are still settling on an identity or what college to attend. I have ex-students who have their own families and I have students who are out of work and struggling. I have lost some to AIDS and drugs while others have just disappeared off the map. I hear from a great many of them and some I never hear from at all. I fill out college and graduate school recommendations. Some of my students have moved to Israel, Britain, the Czech Republic. Often, when students reach their early twenties and are still working at being performers and becoming more acquainted with their talents and skills, I will cast them in one of my adult workshops. I work with young women who have been my students and who now commonly sing in my concerts. Though I never show favoritism while creating a student show, I might decide to go deeper with a student whose talent is obvious, whose passion is genuine, and who in some way may flourish by spending more time working with me.

I might give them jobs as gofers or word processors or assistants who get scripts in order or call various casts and get them to rehearsal on time. They might end up as paid performers, equal to the rest of the professional cast. The relationship depends on the individual and my needs at the time. We would also work on their individual visions for a life in the theater. One of my students wanted to create a one-woman show about being a Mexican Mormon; I watched with pleasure as I saw her material grow and her performances change and expand. At the present time, I'm mentoring a student who wants to use theater technique in his rock band. I'm a little stunned by the raw material but I love the idea and respect my student, so I'm in there helping the musicians take on themes, characters, and dramatic voices. The students who have become teachers and directors themselves ask me for advice on how to handle a scene or individual. I'm not always wise, but it's a good feeling that the ideas that were gifts to me are being passed on to others.

I have loved doing my work with individual ensembles during the last thirty years. The idea that one of my sentences might stay in someone's thoughts and influence someone's actions is thrilling but scary. The power to influence a young person's day-to-day belief system is frightening indeed. Mentoring is complex. I am always careful not to say too much, for there is no one truth about how to be an artist. There's also no proven technique for how to deal with those unique voices inside oneself and the piece of art that gets shaped by their guidance.

I wrote earlier in this book about my sense of wonder and gratitude for those who helped me along the way. What could possibly replace the experience of Henry Brant teaching me 7/8 time by having the two of us dance together up and down a winding staircase? Nothing can equal the moment Ellen Stewart took me into Tom O'Horgan's loft, which was filled with giant gongs and drums of all sizes and shapes, odd-shaped flutes and ancient oboes, so that my idea of music completely changed. I think of Joseph Papp sitting me down and saying, "You can write, Swados." After that I stopped covering up my words and began to speak on paper.

I also remember my frustration when Andrei Serban told me I had to completely rewrite a chorus. And I remember the relief and pride I felt when I finally got it right. Singular tiny moments have had an enormous impact on my life. In public school, one of my fourth-grade teachers had me recite a story out loud; that one recitation got me through most of a rocky year. In the eighth grade, Mrs. Alexander let me write an English assignment in verse. The names and acts of my teachers and directors live inside me and are part of every show I make. I can feel the presence of past generations inside me too, and I take seriously my place in my students' future dreams.

I've said that I believe the theater can heal. When students are fired up enough to express themselves and find form for that expression, the theater can battle the humiliation and horror of a bad home life, problems in a school, or unspoken secret terrors. Often those who become the most smitten by artistic expression are the students you'd never expect to last a day. I've seen this combination of love and salvation bloom often. The teacher grows and discovers, through his or her students, a vast new vocabulary of styles, stories, and forms.

Respect for particular young people keeps a teacher in touch with the ever-changing youth culture, its languages, and its inner music. I don't think that teachers in the arts should freeze in time and in effect be closed to the latest energy in music, poetry, or media. Teaching is a true exchange and, at the end of a project, the teacher should experience a fulfillment similar to that felt by the students. If it hasn't been a risky adventure for the teacher too, the experience hasn't been all that it could have been.

We have to make theater—this powerful and magical art form—more accessible to outsiders as well as those bursting with talent and confidence. You never know what you'll find; there's no predicting. And you never know who's going to find you—and what those young people may bring to enrich your classroom as well as their own lives.

FOR FURTHER READING

HISTORY/REFERENCE

Aronson, Arnold. *American Avant-Garde Theatre: A History*. London: Routledge, 2000. This book is particularly valuable as an overview of the avant-garde theater movement in the United States. Early chapters examine the roots of experimental and avant-garde theater. Later chapters pay close attention to collectives, ritual, and performance art, with specific focus on the Living Theatre, Robert Wilson, Richard Foreman, the Wooster Group, and Reza Abdoh.

Bell, John. "The End of 'Our Domestic Resurrection Circus': Bread and Puppet Theater and Counterculture Performance in the 1990's." *The Drama Review* 43, no. 3, *Puppets, Masks, and Performing Objects* (Autumn 1999): 62–80. This article looks at Bread and Puppet's history, from the early days in New York City to the company's move to Vermont. It focuses on recent changes in the company's legendary summer festivals and its role within its community in Vermont's Northeast Kingdom.

Brook, Peter. *The Empty Space*. New York: Touchstone, 1995. This classic book redefines what theater should be and to what the actor should aspire.

Brown, Helen, and Jane Seitz. "With the Bread and Puppet Theater: An Interview with Peter Schumann." *The Drama Review* 12, no. 2 (Winter 1968): 62–73. Peter Schumann discusses the formation of Bread and Puppet Theater, the inspiration behind it, and the company's mission.

Green, Amy S. *The Revisionist Stage: American Directors Reinvent the Classics*. Cambridge, U.K.: Cambridge University Press, 1994. As the title suggests, this book focuses on experimental interpretations of classic plays and operas. There is a chapter devoted to Greek and Roman plays, one to Shakespeare, one to Molière, and one to Peter Sellars's work with Mozart's operas. In addition to Sellars, the book examines the work of Andrei Serban, Lee Bruer, JoAnne Akalaitis, Richard Schechner, Richard Foreman, and the Flying Karamazov Brothers.

Savran, David. *Breaking the Rules: The Wooster Group*. New York: Theater Communications Group, 1988. David Savran examines the Wooster Group's history from *Routes 1 & 9* to *L.S.D. (. . . Just the High Points . . .)*. He looks not only at the group's history but at their process, the means by which they produced their work. The book includes photos, excerpts from performance texts, and interviews with various members of the Wooster Group.

Schneider, Rebecca, and Gabrielle Cody, eds. *Re:Direction: A Theoretical and Practical Guide*. London: Routledge, 2002. Compiled as a resource for directing students, this volume has a variety of essays and interviews valuable in researching experimental and avant-garde theater. While the first essays in the book concentrate on Stanislavski, Meyerhold, and Brecht, the bulk of the text is dedicated to those who came after, including Peter Brook, Jerzy Grotowski, the Living Theatre, Robert Wilson, Meredith Monk, Richard Foreman, Reza Abdoh, Pina Bausch, the Critical Art Ensemble, Ariane Mnouchkine, the Wooster Group, and Charles Ludlam.

Williams, David. *Peter Brook: A Theatrical Casebook*. London: Methuen, 1988. An overview of Peter Brook's career, starting with his production of *King Lear* and ending with *The Mahabharata*, this book is valuable in examining a life in the theater spanning nearly thirty years. Includes reviews, interviews, notes, and personal accounts from those working with Brook.

GAMES/ACTIVITIES

Boal, Augusto. *Games for Actors and Non-Actors*. Translated by Adrian Jackson. London: Routledge, 1992.

————. *The Rainbow of Desire: The Boal Method of Theatre and Therapy*. Translated by Adrian Jackson. London: Routledge, 1995.

Both of these books elaborate on Boal's Theater of the Oppressed techniques. *Games for Actors and Non-Actors* offers exercises in Image Theater, Invisible Theater, and Forum Theater. *The Rainbow of Desire* focuses on ritual and catharsis, with exercises involving images and masks.

Pasolli, Robert. *A Book on the Open Theater.* Indianapolis: Bobbs-Merrill, 1970. A book of exercises used in the Open Theater, the off-Broadway theater group led by Joseph Chaikin. The book offers information on how the exercises were used in training and rehearsal, and also on their role in performance.

Spolin, Viola. *Improvisation for the Theater: A Handbook of Teaching and Directing Techniques.* 3rd ed. Evanston, Ill.: Northwestern University Press, 1999.

———. *Theater Games for Rehearsal: A Director's Handbook.* Evanston, Ill.: Northwestern University Press, 1985.
Viola Spolin's theater games concentrate on improvisation to engender spontaneity and ensemble building. The third edition of *Improvisation for the Theater* includes notes and new games from her son, Second City founder Paul Sills. *Theater Games for Rehearsal* includes games specifically geared for the rehearsal process, concentrating on preparing the actor for work in front of an audience.

Wangh, Stephen. *An Acrobat of the Heart: A Physical Approach to Acting Inspired by the Work of Jerzy Grotowski.* New York: Vintage Books, 2000. Stephen Wangh relates the training and exercises used when he studied with Jerzy Grotowski. Includes warm-ups as well as physical, vocal, and scene work.

Zaporah, Ruth. *Action Theater: The Improvisation of Presence.* Berkeley, Calif.: North Atlantic Books, 1995. In this book, Ruth Zaporah details the exercises of her twenty-day improvisation training. The exercises have a strong dance/movement bent.